Certified
Christ-based
Sexual Counseling
▪ "The Decade of Sexual Dysfunction" ▪

by Dr. Steven B. DavidSon

Outskirts Press, Inc.
Denver, Colorado

Certified Christ-based Sexual Counseling
"The Decade of Sexual Dysfunction"
All Rights Reserved
Copyright © 2005 Dr. Steven B. DavidSon

Outskirts Press
http://www.outskirtspress.com

ISBN: 1-932672-29-X

Outskirts Press and the "OP" logo are trademarks belonging to Outskirts Press, Inc.

Printed in the United States of America

About the Author

Dr. Steven B. DavidSon is founder of the National Association of Certified Christ-based Counselors in its 12th year. He designed the Christ-based Counseling model, but refers to Jesus as the origin, architect, and empowerment of the Christ-based Counseling framework. Thousands have taken advantage of his works in areas such as marriage, homosexuality, depression, anorexia and bulimia, child discipline, and addiction just to name a few. His Christ-based model is far superior to Christian counseling where often psychology is employed under the guise of sprinkled Scripture text. Dr. Paul Carlin the director and founder of Therapon Institute calls Dr. DavidSon's works the most profound Christ-based concepts he has ever witnessed.

Table of Contents

Christian Couples
Sexually Frustrated Spouses
Singles and
The Homosexually Challenged

Certified Christ-based Sexual Counseling is a counseling guide for couples, sexually frustrated spouses, singles, and the homosexually challenged. Operating from the Christ-based Counseling principles of Balanced Biblical Thinking and Practical Support, the guide provides sound insights, answers tough questions, and offers well-founded support. Topics such as sexual dysfunction, soul-bond, sexual techniques and activities, control and containment, "pornia paranoia" and many others are discussed. Most pastors, preachers, counselors, and counselees will see Jesus relative to sexuality for the first time. No one gives perspective to managing this essential area of our lives like the Master.

Christ-based Counseling Preparation and Distinction

Christ-based Counseling Preparation

Persons who are reading this book are seeking wholeness for one's self or others. There are three functional investments counselees or other participants must make in Christ-based Counseling (CBC) exercises. The participant must:

✓ READ
✓ RESPOND
✓ REITERATE

This means the counselee reads the information, answers each question, and discusses or shares the answers with another person. The questions are divided into blocks of fifty questions each session. The participant can be any person interested in the process (e.g., minister, counselor, friend, relative, etc.).

Whether it is used with or without a Christ-based Counselor, the most effective use of the Christ-based Counseling approach is to begin with the Process of Being Made Whole. I strongly recommend that you complete the Process of Being Made Whole (PBMW) as a prerequisite to the specific counseling needed.

The Process of Being Made Whole, and accompanying course is on the internet at Christbasedcounseling.org. Simply click-on the link or door for the School of Counseling and Certification, and scroll down to The Process of Being Made Whole link. Print out the on-line guide. Use the guide to answer the questions in the on-line course. This on-line course link is the next link beneath the Process of Being Made Whole link.

The Process of Being Made Whole and questions are also included in this book for your convenience. Both the guide and questions are a mirror image of the web versions. If you have completed the Process of Being Made Whole previously, and you have mastered all seven constituents, you may skip the Process of Being Made Whole.

Christ-based Counseling's Distinction

I have counseled literally hundreds of couples and individuals. And unlike the psychological and medical professions, I assure counselees there will be positive change in forty-five days. Persons who meticulously follow each step and who stay-the-course over time may not resolve the issues they face in forty-five days, but there will be change. And they will establish significant progress toward the wholeness they seek. This is because the principles in Christ-based Counseling operate in the angelic realm where the most effective powers and authorities operate to change the physical realm.

Christ-based Counseling is also distinguished from Christian counseling or Christian psychology where the basis is often psychotherapy under the guise of sprinkled scripture text. Christ-based Counseling is based on a sound Scriptural system where the whole approach is thoroughly Biblical.

Finally, this is not a novel, motivational guide, or academic text. This approach is a spiritually empowered process with principles to be observed for the remainder of your life. Typically, the behavior and habits we desire to overcome have been with us for years. Therefore, it may be necessary to review the Christ-based Counseling principles numerous times.

CBC
Liberation and Deliverance Therapy

Preface

The disciples were in awe. Jesus corrected the religious leaders concerning an ancient practice. They were divorcing their wives with regularity and religious impunity (Matt. 19:3-12, NASB). Jesus' authoritative statement concerning this practice and misuse of the Law was, "...in the beginning it was not that way." The disciples who were born and raised in this culture of severing marriage relationships for any cause responded. They perceived Jesus' view as being revolutionary and extraordinarily troublesome. They reasoned that it would be better for a man not to get married (vs. 10).

Jesus admits that all men cannot embrace this truth. Then he provides a startling statement related to the central issue of male-female relationships (i.e., sex), and the disciples ultimate purpose—i.e., leading souls to Christ. Given the disciples' position that it would be better not to marry, Jesus answers as follows:

> *For there are some eunuchs, which were so born from their mother's womb: and there are some eunuchs, which were made eunuchs of men: and there be eunuchs, which have made themselves eunuchs for the*

kingdom of heaven's sake. He that is able to receive it, let him receive it.

If they were not going to marry, and they were going to fulfill their commission, Jesus provided three acceptable possibilities. The first two options were imposed. If a person is born without sexual desire, this would be an extraordinary innate attribute. Like a gifted athlete or musician, it is a God given ability. This person is a eunuch from the womb. The second one is imposed by an authority such as a king. He desires to protect the sanctity of his harem. So, the king surgically removes the male "overseer's" sexual genitalia. This person is a eunuch by the will of men. The final one is a choice. This person denies and avoids personal sexual relations because of his or her pursuit of God's will. This represents the persons who make themselves eunuchs for the kingdom of heaven's sake.

If marriage is too hard, then these are the only other "acceptable" possibilities. The other alternatives result in grave personal and social consequences. Many physical illnesses and virtually all social sicknesses (homicides, illicit drugs, rape, pedophile behavior, sexual dysfunction, broken family structure, forms of mental illness, etc) can be related to the other alternatives. How well we know this today.

Here's the Question

Jesus was a single man. So, which was He? Was He a eunuch from birth? Was He a eunuch from another man's desire? Was He a eunuch for the kingdom of heaven's sake? Or perhaps you believe that He was never confronted with the issue of sex? The answer is provided at the end of this CBC study basis. Be sure to complete this study basis first. May the Lord enrich you through this humble effort.

The Decade of Sexual Dysfunction

If the 1960s were considered the period of the sexual revolution, then this decade could be considered the Decade of Sexual Dysfunction.

Given a culture overwhelmed by sexual innuendo including commercialization, wide spread tolerance and public promiscuity, something is seriously awry. The impression is that this nation is a pillar of sexual prowess. The truth is quite the contrary.

The estimates of men and women suffering with some form of sexual dysfunction in the United States are staggering. It is estimated that about thirty million men, and forty million women suffer some form of sexual dysfunction. Men's symptoms include "erectile" difficulties, pre-mature ejaculation, and loss of desire. Women's issues include loss of desire, lack of lubrication, and inability to reach orgasm[1]. Additionally, it is not politically correct, but homosexuality is a form of sexual dysfunction or sexual disorientation among other serious problems.

Causes range from physiological and psychological conditions to environmental affects. Since there are volumes written on these causes, this document considers the spiritual implications.

---

[1] JAMA 1999 October 6; 282(13): 1229

The Principal Cause for Sexual Dysfunction

Corinthians 6:16, Or do you not know that the one who joins himself to a harlot is one body with her? For He says, "The two will become one flesh."

The Biblical prohibition of extra-marital or pre-marital sex is based on the reality that sexual intercourse has significant and expansive implications on us.

God designed sexuality as the physical ritual, which binds two people spiritually. It is the consummate act, which causes two people to become one. They become deeper embolden with each subsequent encounter.

The power of God's design for sexuality is distorted and desensitized by engaging multiple partners. People have had multiples sex partners for ages. The Bible records plenty of examples of men who had multiple wives. Prostitution also litters Biblical history.

The Jews treated their relationships so cheaply, it became a significant theme of the prophets. Malachi particularly serves notice to those who treated their wives with contempt. They divorced their wives for any conceivable purpose—Malachi 2:13-16. This treacherous behavior did not only affect their marriages, but had further implications on their offspring. Clearly, the true purpose was to become engaged in other relationships.

This promiscuous culture disguised with the cloak of lawfulness caused Jesus to shock these leaders. He knew their true purpose for supporting a culture of divorce, and He informed them that it constituted adulterous behavior (Matthew 5:28).

Later, Jesus made an unconditional proclamation to the religious leaders who widely accepted multiple wives through divorce or polygamy. When they desired to support their behavior by quoting the Law, Jesus said, "…Because of your hardness of heart, Moses permitted you to divorce your wives; but from the beginning it has not been this way." See Deuteronomy 24:1-3; Matthew 19:8, NASB.

Therefore, experience with multiple partners sexually has always been and continues to be a serious spiritual, genetic, and social problem. Perhaps the distinguishing characteristic of our culture is the general practice and acceptance of multiple partners. It is a characteristic that begins with childhood.

It is a reasonable assumption that the majority of persons born in our society will experience more than one person sexually. Whether through divorce and remarriage, or the general acceptance and enticements of our culture, sexual experience with more than one person is the reality. There are exceptions, but they are indeed exceptions.

Furthermore, persons with numerous sexual partners in a short timeframe or simultaneously is not unusual. This is true for both men and women.

While it is not discussed in medical, social, or psychological literature concerning causes for sexual dysfunction, this may be the principal cause. Biblically, the ultimate form of sexual dysfunction is sexual disorientation, or illicit sexual practices with someone other than a person's spouse (I Corinthians 6:13,18; 2 Corinthians 12:21; I Thessalonians 4:3). This is the essence of Jesus words, "in the beginning it was not that way." Mankind was not designed to be in numerous relationships where sex is involved.

Persons who experience numerous sexual partners during their lifetime erode the design and whole purpose of sexuality in committed relationships. This is not to say that these persons do not enjoy the sexual act. However, when they enter marriage where a lasting bond is required, it is not unusual that they cannot respond in the relationship through their marital sex. As soon as the novelty of the relationship fades, the sexual interest does likewise; or the intimacy and depth of the relationship is not improved through the couples' sexual activities. As opposed to operating as the relational "bond-blessing," it becomes a task or chore.

The responses to this condition have always been more plurality and sexual distortion. No wonder the proliferation of adult video, internet pornography, pedophilia, and other forms of sexual deviance are growing exponentially.

Since the Church is a microcosm of society, members of the local church bear the symptoms of this social and spiritual malady.

Believers and Dealing with Sexual Frustration

The wife does not have authority over her own body, but the husband does; and likewise also the husband does not have authority over his own body, but the wife does
(I Corinthians 7:4).

Reflecting the millions of persons suffering with some kind of sexual dysfunction, married couples are not immune to sexual pressure similar to their single counter-parts. This is particularly accurate when one or both suffer some type of sexual dysfunction. Another form of sexual dysfunction is when the couple has incongruent libido. That is, their sex drive is different enough to cause serious frustration in one or both parties. However, this is not new.

Paul in his letter to the Corinthians provides counsel for spouses who live with incongruent libido. His counsel reflects the one flesh principle by reminding couples that their bodies are mutual (I. Corinthians 7:2-4). Based on the text, their mutual cooperation is necessary to control any threats of extra-marital activities. They are commanded to cease any practice, which deprives either mate of sexual needs (vs. 5).

It is interesting. Most of us realize that it requires discipline and practice to excel in any of life's functions. However, concerning sexuality, there is a prevailing attitude that it should be automatic. Everyone should be instantly ready. If a spouse is not on "auto-pilot," there must be something wrong. This was correct in the "beginning" of creation, but it certainly is not true now.

Any act involving physical stamina, skill, timing, and emotional involvement requires good information, self-discipline, cooperation, and practice. This is as true for sexual intimacy as it is for any other endeavor.

A Biblical Perspective on Enhancement

As a loving hind and a graceful doe, Let her breasts satisfy you at all times; Be exhilarated always with her love (Proverbs 5:19).

There are numerous books, guides, and other resources on improving sex life. It is demanding physically, so spouses need to develop and maintain good physical conditioning. Hygiene is a factor in most cases. Good appearance can be a factor. Communicating about what is and is not pleasurable sexually is necessary. The range of conditions, which support a great marital sex life is exhaustive.

Therefore, this document discusses a Biblical view along with some other obvious considerations.

First, the marriage bed is undefiled. Any sex outside of the spiritual, physical, and "soulish" commitment represented by marriage is by definition, defiled.

Sex is not inherently evil. Sex is not wicked, perverse or as some would define it, "nasty." No couple has the "platform" to experience sexuality to its fullest like a couple in Christ.

There is a worldly saying concerning sexuality. "If you want good sex, don't get married." Obviously, Satan is the origin of this lie. Given the full support of the almighty God and His heavenly principalities, "You have never had great sex, until you are married in Christ."

However, spouses must employ some important and powerful principles concerning sexual intimacy.

Pray for Great Sex

Believers need to ask God to enhance their sexual relations. Some people act as if it is a sin to ask God to enhance their sex. This is from the under pinning that something is wrong with sex. We often forget, God CREATED sexual intimacy. Among many things such as wisdom, eternal life, and fellowship with Him, the term abundant life also means to have a rich sexual life with one's spouse.

During the counseling experience, I direct couples to pray daily that God will make them the husband or wife of Ephesians 5, and Colossians 3. Likewise, spouses should ask the Lord to grant the ability to identify and respond to a respective spouse's sexual needs.

Prepare for Great Sex

Well before the actual act is initiated, it also involves emotional support and appreciation. This means that couples who become great supporters of each other are more likely to enjoy an excellent sex life.

Fun and Adventure

One day my wife called me at work, and said she had a surprise for me when I arrived home. It was not a birthday or anniversary, she just desired to surprise me. Actually, I did not think about it during the day, and I had no idea what she planned. I entered my home through the garage as usual. I was greeted by our dog in the garage, and when I opened the door to enter the home, "lo and behold." My wife was standing before me. She was wearing a physician's white smock. The smock was long enough to cover the subject, but short and revealing enough to make my heart skip a beat. She had on high-healed shoes, and fish net stockings. She also had a stethoscope around her neck. She said, "Dr. DavidSon, what would you like me to examine today." I replied, "Lord have mercy." Like a good old-fashion movie, I will leave the remainder to your imagination.

The typical believer is almost fearful to ask what kinds of things are Biblically acceptable sexually. While the Bible clearly expresses the need for marriage, it is categorically and contextually quiet on what married couples can do sexually. I say categorically and contextually because, there is no place where sexual techniques within marriage are discussed. This does not mean that some writers do not attempt to force a restrictive view upon the Bible, which is not there. If God was concerned about sexual techniques, He would have placed them in the Bible. He clearly is not as "restrictive" as we are. So, here I have listed five Bible-based, "soul-bond" principles that I share with married couples concerning sexual techniques in the context of marriage:

Spiritual Consciousness: Christian spouses can enjoy any technique or attraction that does not violate their personal faith or consciousness about the activity (Romans 8:14-21; 22-23). If a spouse has a sense of guilt or regret, then the act or activity is sin to the spouse and relationship.

Relational Implications: If it is an activity, which adversely affects a spouse, or others in the family mentally, physically, or spiritually, it is probably an activity that would be prohibited Biblically (Romans 15:1-3).

Pleasure via Pain: If it is an activity whereby pleasure is achieved by inflicting or receiving pain, it would not be Biblically acceptable. Pain is the direct result of sin (Genesis 3:16), and sexuality was not created as an instrument of pain (Genesis 1:26-28). It was created for fruitfulness (i.e., relational depth and bonding) and filling the earth. If a spouse experiences pain during coitus, the couple should seek medical assistance.

Violation of Public Law: The activity cannot be a violation of public law (Romans 13:1-7). Acts that are against the law such as lewd or lascivious public conduct would be Biblically prohibited. Close attention must be given here. There could be state or local laws, which prohibit some activities couples routinely practice.

Maintain the Sanctity of the Relationship: The sanctity of the relationship must be maintained through the act or activity. Sanctity means the oneness, intimacy, and privacy. This underscores the very meaning of the "one-flesh" principle stated by Jesus (Genesis 2:24; Matthew 19:6). Among other issues, this is the principal problem with viewing pornographic material for sexual arousal. Typically, pornographic materials involve other persons (e.g., views of other women or men).

Questions and Comments Concerning Enhancement

Believers who know of the bonding principles have posed several questions and hearsay.

"Autopornography:" Knowing these principles, a believer asked, "is it a problem if the pornographic material was 'autopornographic?'" That is, what if the married couple recorded and viewed themselves? It did not appear to violate any of the principles. I responded, "I would hate for that tape to get into the hands of someone else." Obviously, it would be sin for me. Also, producing an "autopornographic" recording could be against local or state law.

Sexual Limits in the Songs of Solomon: Another believer who knew of these principles stated that she heard there were limits. She said it was found in the Songs of Solomon. Again, a thorough search of Scripture does not reveal any such limits. Certainly the Songs of Solomon have romantic and sensual overtones representing physical attraction. However, the passages—while using physical descriptions--are not about sexuality per se, and the text certainly is not designed as a direct or indirect limit on sexual activities within <u>marriage</u>.

Sex and the Forbidden Fruit: There are some persons who believe the forbidden fruit in the Garden of Eden was not what it seems. They propose that the forbidden fruit was actually a metaphor for forbidden types of sex between the first man and woman. Another view is that Satan had intercourse with Eve, and this is what constituted the forbidden fruit. Both of these, and any similar views are seriously flawed. They represent metaphoric or allegoric forms of interpretation.

Unless it is otherwise stated or implied in the passage, the Bible is interpreted literally. As an example, Jesus' reference to living water and many similar illustrations were metaphors. However, it is clear in the respective passage that He is using a metaphor. Often, He uses an earthly metaphor to illustrate a spiritual reality.

Persons viewing accounts in Genesis as metaphoric or allegoric are doing so without any contextual support, and to maintain consistency all of the events in creation must be viewed similarly. Given their view, nothing is what it seems in the first chapters of Genesis. The first day is not the first day. The sun is not the sun. The stars are not stars, and forbidden fruit is not forbidden fruit. Given these forms of interpretation, all of these represent something else. Unfortunately, the man is also not a man, and the woman is not actually a woman. As anyone can see, these forms of interpretation undermine the whole book of Genesis. Clearly, the writer of Genesis—Moses—gives no indication that the passage is to be viewed metaphorically. This underscores the danger of attempting to force one's view concerning sexual limits upon the Biblical text.

The bottom-line of Scripture concerning sex is marriage. If the couple is married, sex is designed to plunge each spouse deeper into oneness. This is the essence of soul-bonding. No couple should, and no couple can enjoy sex like a Christian couple. Sexual immorality does not exist within the bounds of marriage--as shown within the soul-bonding principles. Remember, the marriage bed is not defiled (Hebrews 13:4).

Sexuality and the Believer, Control and Containment

Control and containment are spiritual requisites. These two descriptive terms are synonymous, and they clearly represent the importance of living lives free of sexual immorality. This is the point. Believers need to use wisdom to determine what they can do to avoid sexual immorality.

Possessing His Vessel, and Commentator's Pornia-paranoia

That each of you know how to possess his own vessel in sanctification and honor
(I Thessalonians 4:4).

I Thessalonians 4:4 is one of those feared passages. Most commentators wrestle with the meaning of the term, "possess his own vessel." Some suggest that men need to control themselves by finding a wife, or controlling a wife. Other commentators suggest that it means to control one's body. Both of these interpretations underscore an obvious fear, and as a result these and similar renderings do little to help believers.

Biblical teachers, preachers, and others warn believers to abstain from sexual immorality. This is the correct Biblical position. However, it is always a functional error to tell people what they should not do, but fail to consider what they can do. This is particularly true in the area of sexuality. I have been as guilty in this regard as anyone else. The major fear is that we will encourage people to do something that may appear taboo. I call this, "pornia-paranoia." Pornia is the Greek term often translated immorality in the New Testament. And typically it refers to sex related immorality.

Many church leaders are so afraid to discuss what believers can do to control themselves, they avoid any consideration. After years of counseling, I have discovered that this vacuum is exploited by Satan. It leaves believers uncertain about activities they use to relieve themselves. They are faced with a sense of guilt and confusion. Clearly, this "pornia-paranoia" results in a lack of wisdom. It further represents cowardice on our part, and I do not believe our Savior is pleased.

Proposing that the text means merely to acquire a wife excludes an enormous segment of other believers. What about those who have wives, but they are sexually frustrated? What about wives who are sexually frustrated? What about single men? What about single females? Limiting the term to possessing a wife is an extraordinarily narrow view of the term. What about those who propose the text means for believers to control their bodies? Certainly, this seems to be the view that represents all believers. However, the question is how? How do they control their bodies? This is where the answers stop.

One of the most difficult challenges to the frustrated spouse, or single believer is being sexually functional to any degree, but abstaining from illicit sexual encounters. These believers find this to be one of the most troubling difficulties in their walk with the Lord.

The Romans 7 road of "doing what they desire not to do, and not doing what they desire to do" is not so acute as when it relates to sex.

Single believers particularly, battle in every conceivable way. Others do not battle at all. They simply go with the flow. This is very unfortunate. Nevertheless, this guide attempts to discuss what believers can do.

But if they do not have self-control, let them marry; for it is better to marry than to burn
(1 Corinthians 7:9).

While this section is devoted to singles, it is helpful for frustrated spouses who must use similar strategies.

A Cause for Marriage

Wisdom dictates that singles not date or socially entertain persons who do not meet minimal expectations. Again, this is where our culture is notorious for clichés such as "go with the flow," "casual sex," and "booty call." As demonstrated in the aforementioned, there is no such thing as casual sex. It is a term concocted by Satan.

Even in circumstances when it is obvious that a person is not companionship worthy, it is not unusual that believers will maintain a relationship with a person who has sexual or amorous intentions.

Unfortunately, the sexual attraction or companionship drive is so powerful it often exceeds good judgment, and intellectual caution.

This is a precursor to disaster. Many adults know within a conversation or single date, whether a person possesses essential companionship qualities.

Clearly, there are persons who have no standards. These persons accept all comers. Obviously, this study is not devoted to persons suffering with extreme forms of the Devil's Deception and Desperation Disorder (4D).

Nevertheless, once the sexual vice has yoked the believer's life with an undesirable companionship partner, it requires a major undertaking to loose the believer from the established soul-bond.

It is just as unfortunate when a person enters sexual encounters so often and readily, that one is able to move swiftly into subsequent relationships. Relationships and the accompanying sexual experience resemble a revolving door, "one person in another person out, next."

Often these persons become married, which plunges the couple into a commitment before God that causes extreme relational suffering. Unfortunately, when two adults decide they will marry as opposed to discontinuing their sexual relationship, this subsequent decision can be worse than the decision to enter a sexual relationship.

Observing the principle stated in I Corinthians 7:9, it is understood that persons experiencing a loss of control are doing so with a worthy marital candidate. If not, the sexual activity must be terminated. Otherwise, marriage is the appropriate response.

Balanced Biblical Thinking and Practical Therapy

What can the believer do? The single believer who is sexually functional and companionship worthy needs every advantage possible. It involves prayer, right thinking, and numerous other activities.

Resisting Chains vs. Breaking Chains

Simply stated, resisting temptation--while difficult at times-- is easier than breaking the bondage of sin. Consider a shackle, which is a steel brace attached to a chain. It is less difficult to keep one's arm out of the shackle than attempting to break the shackle once it is locked.

As difficult as resisting sex sin may be, once a believer is trapped, only God can deliver the believer from the entrapment. And it is not unusual that the believer has to be delivered through some kind of unpleasant experience (Hebrews 12:5-11). So, the first line of defense is not to begin the activity in the first place. Never accept the "only once" attraction to sin. This is all Satan needs to shackle a believer. Sin – by definition – does not allow for a, "one time only" encounter. Unless intervention is employed, sin is designed to draw, capture, and kill every time (James 1:15).

When the serpent encounters the woman in the Garden of Eden, he does not unveil his whole scheme. He only wants the woman to eat of the tree one time (Genesis 3:1-6). Compare her response to Jesus' response in His wilderness experience. Again, Satan offers a series of temptations. One by one, Jesus overcomes each of them (Matthew 4:4-11). Each time Jesus uses the Word of God. This is discussed later in greater detail. An amazing thing happens after Jesus resists Satan's temptation. Satan departs and angels minister to Jesus. Luke, in his account of Satan's temptation of Jesus adds a reminder of Satan's persistence (Luke 4:13). Luke adds, "…he departed from him for a [season]." Satan is going to return, but if we resist Satan, he'll flee (James 4:7). Often, believers do not resist him. Once there is no resistance, he becomes a resident in that area of our lives. Eventually, the sin spreads like cancer and dominates us completely.

Thought Management

It is imperative that believers maintain a full slate of conscientious activities. These activities should revolve around family and church life, personal health, and spiritual development. Christians-- married and single-- must be where they are supposed to be, and do what they are supposed to do. Many Christians testify that when they have altered their schedule due to boredom or lack of interest, they have encountered the beginning of problems.

Spiritual Consecration

Singleness offers an excellent period to enter a life of service and consecration that is difficult for married couples to experience (I Corinthians 7:7-8; 32-34). It is an excellent period to enter in-depth studies of God's Word and related activities, particularly if the single person does not have children. Nevertheless, spiritual consecration is still required.

Self-relief Therapy

Even with all singles do, the combination of companionship desires and sex drive can be overwhelming. Given the adverse and pervasive impact of an ill-advised relationship, it is preferable to use self-induced forms of relief. Singles and sexually frustrated spouses should do all they can to abstain from a sexual encounter with another person. Perhaps, this is what Paul meant when he said, "if you cannot contain or control yourself... "(I Corinthians 7:9), and "possess his own vessel" (I Thessalonians 4:4).

Containment and possessing one's own vessel involves every means necessary to avoid sexual relations with another person or being. However, the sanctity of oneness must always be maintained. This means to avoid pornographic materials, or other forms of relief, which exploit other persons or beings (Leviticus 18:6-23). One final caution concerns fantasy. Fantasy involving another person as the object can be the beginning of the James 1:15 process (i.e., lust, sin, death). Both married couples and singles must be careful about the focus of fantasies.

Perhaps the most accurate rendering of "possessing his own vessel" means to control our sexual organs. Jesus recognized that our bodily functions and organs (e.g., eye, hand, minds, etc.) often operated against our personal well-being. His view was to take drastic actions against those parts of our anatomy if they caused us to stumble (Matthew 18:7-8). While I am not suggesting anything as drastic, self-induced forms of sexual relief have the same purpose as plucking an eye, or severing a hand.

As discussed concerning sexual techniques for couples, the Bible outlines sexual prohibitions in great detail. However, it does not address sexual techniques, and likewise it does not address forms of self-relief. The forms of self-relief were clearly left to the believer.

Jesus and Sexuality, Principles for All Believers

No guide could be extolled as being Christ-based without viewing the central topic from a Life of Christ perspective. Jesus is the Master teacher, and standard of excellence. His examples on dealing with sexuality are priceless.

A True Story

It was the fall of 1978. I sold and purchased income property, and I was conducting a lot of business with an employment-related credit union. Professionally, I knew the loan officers and tellers. It was a gorgeous Friday afternoon in San Francisco, and I made a deposit with one of the tellers. During our cordial exchange, she asked me what I would be doing for the weekend. I told her my family was gone to Houston, and I was going to be visiting my old buddies. She replied, "oh, you are going out on the town" or something very similar. I told her it was not like that. Before handing me the deposit receipt, I noticed her write something on it.

After a parting pleasantry and exiting the office, I read what she had scribbled. It was her phone number with a little note to call her. I was floored to say the least. The blinders were off. This was an open door to an affair. My ego was thoroughly inflated. I was amused, impressed, and absolutely tempted. However, within hours I knew what to do. I simply threw the number away, and I would not return to the credit union unless it was absolutely necessary. Unfortunately, I was in for a major surprise, and a horrific seven-day period. Friday evening I met with my friends as scheduled, and I do not recall going into any detail about what occurred earlier in the day.

Saturday was a typical day, but shortly after midnight I was awaken by a phone call. It was the woman at the credit union.

She wanted to know why I had not called, and I explained. I tried to do so without insulting her. I expressed to her that she was attractive and personable, but I was married. She replied, "don't you know, I know you are married." She promised me that she would not interfere with my family.

She knew all about me, and I would discover that she knew more than what was disclosed on file at the credit union. She was almost ten years older than I, and her marriage was on the rocks. She spoke about her spouse and children. She knew my wife's name, and my children. Each night she would call me.

Once I could see that the family angle would not work, I used the ministry angle. I thought I would try to say the most repulsive thing I could think. So, I recall asking her, "Could you imagine having sexual relations with a married minister?" She replied, "I think that would be angelic." I knew I was in serious trouble.

Therefore, in my desperation I called for a meeting of the elders—my two childhood buddies. I did not tell them much the previous Friday when we were together, but when they arrived I told them the details. I wanted their advice on what to do. Ironically, they were not as spiritual as I was at that time in our lives. However, they both were absolutely firm that I should do whatever necessary to end the communication.

I acted upon their counsel. The next time she called, I told her that she had to discontinue the calls. She said that I would have to tell her in person. I refused. She threatened to visit my home. Although she lived in a different city, she knew exactly where I lived. She described the home in detail. I knew I could not allow her to visit my home. There was an elderly couple who lived across the street in front of our home. Their front door was always open, and they watched street activity intently through their screen door. All I needed was a woman creating a scene in front of my home.

Any temptation was replaced by fear. I agreed to meet her in a public place. I met her at a park in the city where she lived. We arranged to meet on a vacant baseball diamond. I knew the area because I played softball there. It was evening, but usually the field lamps lit the diamond. However, when I arrived the lights were off. I saw her at a distance. She was lying on the dug-out bench. I approached her, and simply repeated what I told her on the phone. I asked her to return to her car, and for her safety I would run around the park a few times. As I ran, I could see she would not return to her car. After the final lap, I got in my car and returned home.

Later, I received another phone call. She wanted to know why I left her there. A day or so later, I told her that there had been an emergency, and my wife was returning home early. Yes, I confess, I was not truthful. She promised she would not call me any more, and asked me not to report her for using my personal information. Although I saw her at the credit union, she never bothered me again.

Jesus, A Single Man Conquers Sexual Temptation

After this experience, I began searching the Life of Jesus for a related experience. I knew He was tempted in every area of His life (Hebrews 4:15). However, I never saw or heard how He was tempted sexually. It was during this experience that I discovered a different view of Jesus and the woman at the well.

Jesus and the Woman at the Well

I was astonished when I viewed the experience from a male-female perspective. Jesus' encounter with the Samaritan woman provides spouses and singles with excellent principles on overcoming the potential for sexual exploitation of others and one's self.

I found several facts apparent in the passage (John 4:1-29). The writer—Apostle John-- informs us as follows:

John 4	Conversational Exchange
Verse 6	He was tired and sitting by a well.
Verse 7	A woman came to the well.
Verse 7	Jesus initiates the conversation.
Verse 8	The writer informs the reader, the disciples were not there.
Verse 9	The woman was startled by the questions.
Verse 9	The woman recognized his status as a Jew.
Verse 10	Jesus reverses thought from the requester to the provider.
Verse 10	Jesus offers something superior.
Verse 11	The woman asks deeper and more probing questions.
Verse 12	The woman asks another status question.
Verse 13	Jesus never responds directly to the status question.
Verse 15	The woman requests the water.
Verse 16	Jesus changes the conversation completely, calling for her husband.
Verse 17	She replies that she does not have a husband.
Verse 18	Jesus already knows about the husbands and other details.
Verse 19	She perceives He is a prophet. She uses a spiritual term for the first time.

Note that Jesus was tired. We are most vulnerable to poor decision making when we are tired or otherwise incapacitated. This emphasizes the importance of prayer and rest. If I continued to allow the phone calls and conversations, eventually I would have failed due to emotional wear and changing circumstances.

Jesus was by himself. His disciples were not there. We are also more likely to become involved in something inappropriate if there is some measure of secrecy. The woman at the credit union sensed the perfect time to inform me of her interest. My family was gone.

Consider that the well was a public meeting place. It was a place where men met women (Genesis 24:12-21; 29:1-12; Exodus 2:15-17). This is how I met the woman.

This woman at the well was curious and status conscience. My friends' view was that the woman at the credit union knew about my finances, and this contributed to her interest.

The woman at the well was despised, particularly by Jews. So she was surprised by Jesus' question. While some commentators believe the woman had an "attitude" or a bit of rudeness, the weight of the evidence does not support such a position. Based on her questioning, the status she could assume was paramount in her thinking. The woman finally asks for the "water." No one knows what she expected, but we do know that she was not pursuing spiritual water. She has no idea that Jesus was speaking of spiritual matters.

Jesus completely changes the conversation. Jesus inquires about her husband when he already knows that she does not have a husband. The actual rendering of the text is "go call your man." Her reply is, "I do not have a man." Clearly, there was a man in her life, but she decided to lie. She was opening the door to a relationship with Jesus.

Jesus responds that she has in-fact told the truth. While she is lying, she has had several relationships, but she has never had oneness with any man. It seems to imply that she is constantly moving through relationships. Therefore, she truly did not have a man. Jesus reveals six relationships. It is only after He reveals her numerous relationships that she recognizes, He is a spiritual authority. She suggests that Jesus is a prophet. Now, she is on the same plane as Jesus, and she begins to ask spiritual questions. Ultimately, she meets Jesus as the Savior of her life.

The evidence is convincing that she was viewing Jesus as a potential lover. Jesus knew exactly what her intentions would be when He initiated the conversation. Thus, he moved right to the heart of her intentions when He asked about her man.

Moreover, it could have been a historic disaster if Jesus capitulated. How did he overcome? Jesus demonstrated a primary principle when engaging persons of the opposite sex. I call this, "soul over sex" or SOS. He was more concerned about the emptiness in their souls or their spiritual needs. He never wavered between their most significant need versus their temporal needs. More importantly, He never wavered between His eternal responsibility and any personal sexual desires He possessed.

It is virtually impossible for a believer to lead an unbeliever to Christ, while having sex with the unbeliever—unless they are already married (I Corinthians 7:12-14). Likewise, it is self-defeating for one believer to encourage another believer's development in Christ, while both believers are engaged in extra-marital, or pre-marital sex. First, they need to terminate the sexual activities or marry. The believer's ministry and purpose must be held in higher regard than one's sexual or companionship desires.

Three Other Encounters with Sexual Implications

The Bible records at least three other recorded instances where Jesus was involved in experiences where his desire to save souls overcame any sexual overtones.

The woman who was all over Jesus: The first is in Luke 7:37-48 where a woman enters a Pharisee's home to minister to Jesus. She approaches Jesus from behind, and washes his feet with her tears and perfume. She also kisses his feet. Imagine! I am personally aware of pastors, counselors, and others who have fallen prey to their own sexual indiscretions under less imposing circumstances. The response of the Pharisee, Simon, is noteworthy. Upon observing this intimate exchange and cultural rite, he reasons that Jesus could not be a prophet. If Jesus were a prophet, he certainly would know what kind of person was "touching" Him. Obviously, Jesus appreciated the woman's affection. Simon concludes, she is a sinner. Referring to her as a sinner was a religious description. What Simon actually meant is that she was a woman of the streets. She was unworthy of being considered as a mate. As Simon would have it, she would not even be able to "touch" him (i.e., Simon). However, Jesus is more concerned about her soul than companionship or sex.

She does it again: Again, in John 12:1-8 most agree that it is the same woman, but a later date. She ministers to Jesus in a very similar way. This time Judas envies the expenditure of perfume. Again, Jesus is so focused on His purpose, there is not the slightest indication of slipping on his part sexually. His focus is on the cross.

Wild in the wilderness: Finally, there is Jesus' wilderness experience (Matthew 4:1-11). While this is earlier in the life of Jesus than the aforementioned experiences, the sexual encounter is not so easily discernable, but it is not difficult to envision it. Satan tempts Jesus in three areas. He begins with food. Satan never begins his temptation with his full intention. He begins with a light approach. He increases the intensity with each subsequent attempt. Recognizing that Jesus is hungry (vs. 2), Satan does not merely tempt Jesus to change stones into bread. Satan attempts to stir Jesus' ego as a psychological factor along with His physical hunger. Satan begins his temptation with the challenge, "if you are the Son of God?" Jesus responds with God's Word, "man does not live by bread alone, but by every word that proceeds from the mouth of God." Jesus does not even discuss the issue of whether He is God's Son.

Again, Satan attacks Jesus. This time Satan takes his cue from Jesus. Since Jesus used God's Word to foil Satan's initial attempt, Satan laces his second temptation with God's Word. Upon the top of the temple, Satan attempts to strike at Jesus' ego by questioning His relationship as the Son of God. This time Satan wants Jesus to jump down with the assurance that God will deliver Him (Psalms 91:10-11)--if He is the Son of God. Jesus answers Satan with the Word of God. Jesus knows that His personal desire must not impose upon God's desire. Jesus responds, "You shall not put the Lord your God to the test."

Clearly, Satan is loosing the battle. Therefore, his final "wilderness" temptation would be an all out attack. Satan appeals to the "deadly three" (i.e., lust of the flesh, lust of the eyes, and pride of life--see 1. John 2:16). He takes Jesus to a high mountain, and shows Jesus all the kingdoms of the world and their glory. Although Satan began with an indirect attack concerning an appeal to turn stones into bread, Satan's ultimate purpose was for Jesus to worship him. This is what Satan desired beginning with the first temptation. Jesus defeats Satan again.

So, where is the sexual temptation? When Satan showed Jesus all of the kingdoms and their glory, it means Jesus saw every detail of "glory." The list would include silver, gold, armies, palaces, servants, fame, power and authority. Based on the Biblical record of persons who possessed such wealth and authority, no doubt Jesus saw harems with the most gorgeous women ever to walk this planet. As an example, Jesus' ancestor Solomon became woman "crazy." He took full advantage of more than one-thousand women who turned his heart from God (I. Kings 11:3). Jesus responds to Satan's offer with His most fierce and personal rebuke,"... Begone, Satan! For it is written, 'You shall worship the Lord your God, and serve Him only'"(vs. 10, NASB). The believer can likewise respond to every scheme of Satan.

When All Else Fails

When it comes to sexual improprieties in the life of a believer, David is probably cited most often. His adultery and accompanying murder is well chronicled (2. Samuel 11:3-17). As a counselor, I do not often encounter persons who are dealing with both adultery and murder in their lives. However, I often speak with singles whom battle sexual temptations related to their singleness. I have also worked with spouses in the clutches of adultery, and I have experienced both of them (i.e., extra-marital, pre-marital) directly or indirectly (James 5:16).

This guide clearly explains the implications of extra marital or pre-marital sex. It goes without saying that both of them have devastating influence on us personally, and our society as a whole.

Moreover, no sin should be "marginalized." This is not an attempt to "marginalize" any sin. However, most believers have not engaged in the level of debauchery demonstrated by David.

No doubt, David thought he was going to die the moment Nathan revealed David's sin (2 Samuel 12:1-13). The Law called for the death of an adulterer or murderer (Leviticus 20:10; Numbers 35:31). However, upon David's confession that He sinned Nathan makes a startling announcement, "The Lord has taken away your sin" (v. 13). Moreover, God blesses David and Bathsheba with a son, Solomon, who is a fore parent of Jesus. This experience along with countless others demonstrates the depth and degree of God's love for His children. God's love is greater than our own self-condemnation.

> *We shall know by this that we are of the truth, and shall assure our heart before Him, in whatever our heart condemns us; <u>for God is greater than our heart, and knows all things</u>*
> *(I John 3:19-20).*

God knew that David loved Him. No act or repeated acts can erase God's love for the believer (Romans 8:35-39). "Many are the afflictions of the righteous, but God delivereth him out of them all (Psalms 34:19)."

Certainly, believers suffer the circumstances of their behavior (Galatians 6:7-8), and each believer should take every step necessary to overcome any sin. Deliverance from sexual sin as with most vices requires a process. It could be lengthy and it will probably be painful, but God will deliver his children. He always does.

Therefore, when all else fails, the believer must readily and repeatedly turn to the Lord as often as necessary. I have no greater counsel than those penned by the Apostle John:

> *If we confess our sins, He is faithful and righteous to forgive us our sins and to cleanse us from all unrighteousness*
> *(I John 1:9).*

May the Lord richly bless!
sbd

Counselor's Answer

CAUTION: You are not to read this answer unless you have read the study in its entirety.

Is Jesus a eunuch from His mother's womb? I do not believe so. Is Jesus a eunuch from a King? I do not believe so. Is he a man who abstained from sex for the kingdom of heaven's sake? I believe this has to be the answer.

Jesus could not hold himself to be the advocate of mankind if He did not have sexual ability (I John 2:1). He truly does not intimately know our frame if He did not have sexual desires (Psalms 103:14). If Jesus was not tempted sexually, He was not tempted in all ways (Hebrews 4:15). Given the impact and reality of sexuality upon the human race, it is unimaginable that God's Son would be devoid of a primary human characteristic. There is no doubt in my mind that Jesus had sexual desire. However, humanity sounded an SOS distress signal, and He stayed the course. He preferred our souls over sex.

Program
Tools

Session Questions

Foreword

1. Who did Jesus correct?

2. What were these religious leaders doing to their wives?

3. What did Jesus say about this practice?

4. How did the disciples perceive Jesus' view?

5. What did the disciples reason?

6. What is one of the central issues between males and females?

7. What is the believers/disciples ultimate purpose?

8. What did Jesus say concerning the disciples reasoning that it would be better not to marry?

9. What did Jesus mean by a person who was a eunuch from his mother's womb?

10. What did Jesus mean by a person who becomes a eunuch by men?

11. What did Jesus mean by a person who becomes a eunuch for the kingdom of heaven's sake?

12. What is the likely result of any other alternative than those identified by Jesus?

13. Since Jesus was a single man, which was he? (refer to questions 9 – 10)

The Decade of Sexual Dysfunction

14. What is the decade of the 1960s called?

15. What might this decade be called?

16. Give the estimates on men and woman suffering with some form of sexual dysfunction?

17. What are some of the men's issues of dysfunction?

18. What are some of the women's issues of dysfunction?

19. What else is a form of sexual dysfunction?

The Principal Cause for Sexual Dysfunction

20. What did God design sexuality to do?

21. How is God's design for sexuality distorted and desensitized?

22. Does the Bible record plenty of examples of men who had multiple wives? If so, give an example of at least one person (Biblical insight question).

23. Who treated their relationships cheaply?

24. Which prophet served notice on those persons who divorced their wives for any conceivable reason?

25. What was their true purpose for divorcing their wives?

26. After ages of this practice, how did Jesus shock these leaders?

27. What did Jesus tell these leaders when they explained that Moses allowed divorce?

28. What continues to be a serious spiritual, genetic, and social problem?

29. What is the distinguishing characteristic of our culture?

30. What is a reasonable assumption about the majority of persons born in our society?

31. How is it that we experience more than one person sexually?

32. What also happens within short time frames or simultaneously with numerous people?

33. Biblically, what is the ultimate form of sexual dysfunction?

34. According to Jesus, how many persons was man designed to be involved with sexually? And what term does he use to emphasize this fact?

35. What happens to persons who experience numerous sexual partners?

36. Upon entering marriage, what is often the case for persons who have had several sexual partners?

37. What happens when the novelty of the marriage fades?

38. As opposed to operating as the relational bond blessing, what does sexuality become in the relationship?

39. Due to the pervasive and growing trend of sexual dysfunction, and overall degrading of sexuality, what has proliferated?

40. Has this condition had an effect on the Church?

Believers and Dealing with Sexual Frustration

41. Do [...] odies? Where wou [...] ?

42. Wh[...] erning sp[...]

43. Wh[...]

44. Wh[...] ent libido?

45. Why[...]

46. Wh[...] ation for sexu[...]

47. What is required for any act, sexual or otherwise requiring physical stamina, skill, timing, and emotional involvement?

48. Are there numerous books and guides on improving sexual intimacy?

49. Given the Biblical perspective, what is stated about the marriage bed?

50. By definition what IS defiled?

51. Is sex inherently evil? Is it wicked? Is it nasty?

52. Who has the right to experience sexuality to its fullest?

53. What is a worldly saying concerning sex and marriage?

54. Who is the origin of this saying?

55. Who fully supports Christian married couples and great sexual intimacy?

56. What is the first principle concerning sexual intimacy?

57. Concerning creation, why would couples pray for God to enhance their sexual intimacy?

58. How do couples prepare for greater sexual intimacy?

59. Read the story of Mrs. DavidSon's creative idea. Why would her idea and activities enhance the relationship with her husband?

60. What is the typical believer fearful to ask?

61. Does the Bible discuss what married couples can do sexually?

62. Are there persons who attempt to place a restrictive view on what couples can do?

63. How many Bible-based soul-bond principles does Dr. DavidSon recommend?

64. Explain Spiritual Consciousness.

65. Explain Relational Implications.

66. Explain Pleasure via Pain.

67. Explain Violation of Public Law.

68. Explain Maintaining the Sanctity of the Relationship.

69. Why is using pornographic material (e.g., video, magazines, etc.) to cause sexual arousal a problem for couples?

70. What is "autopornography"?

71. Although "autopornography" did not appear to violate any of the soul-bond principles, how could it become a problem?

72. Does any of the text in the Songs of Solomon specifically relate to limitations on sex within the bounds of marriage?

73. What do some people believe the forbidden fruit represents in the Garden of Eden?

74. What forms of interpretation might lead a person to believe that the forbidden fruit represents forbidden forms of sex between two Christian spouses?

75. Unless otherwise stated or implied by the Biblical text, how is the Bible interpreted?

76. Who often used metaphors when he taught?

77. What are people doing who view Genesis as metaphoric or allegoric?

78. Given their view, is a day a day? Is the sun the sun? Are the stars the stars?

79. Given their view, what are the other problems concerning man and woman?

80. What does this form of interpretation do to the Book of Genesis?

81. What is the bottom-line of Scripture concerning sex?

82. What does sexual intimacy do for the married couple?

83. Does sexual immorality exist within the bounds of marriage— as shown within the soul-bond principles?

Sexuality and the Believer, Control and Containment

84. What do control and containment represent?

85. Give two suggestions commentators provide for the meaning of "possess his own vessel."

86. What do Biblical teachers and counselors warn believers concerning sexual immorality?

87. What is the "functional error"?

88. What is the major fear?

89. What is pornia?

90. There is such fear, what do leaders often neglect?

91. How does this neglect leave believers?

92. If the clause, "possess his own vessel" only refers to obtaining or controlling a wife, what is the obvious problem with such a view?

93. What is the weakness if the meaning is for believers to control their bodies?

94. What is one of the most difficult challenges for frustrated spouses and single believers?

95. Concerning singles, what does wisdom dictate?

96. Concerning sex, name a few notorious clichés.

97. Who is the origin of the term, casual sex?

98. What do believers practice even when it is obvious that a person is not companionship worthy?

99. What often exceeds good judgment, and intellectual caution?

100. What do most adults recognize within a conversation or a single date?

101. Once a believer is sexually yoked (i.e., soul-bond) with a person lacking companionship qualities, what is required to loose the believer?

102. What is as unfortunate as becoming yoked (i.e., soul-bond) with a person who lacks companionship qualities?

103. What often occurs to persons who lack companionship qualities, but they plunge into marriage?

104. What is understood about Paul's counsel to couples who cannot control themselves sexually (I. Corinthians 7:9)?

105. What kind of activities is the believer involved who is sexually functional and companionship worthy?

106. What is less difficult, resisting sin or breaking the bondage of sin?

107. Once a believer is trapped, who is the only source of deliverance?

108. What kind of experience can a believer expect who is trapped in sexual related sin (Heb. 12:5-11)?

109. What is the first line of defense concerning sex related sin?

110. What mental scheme must the believer refuse to accept?

111. Does sin allow a one time only experiment? Explain.

112. Unless intervention occurs, what is sin designed to do?

113. Does the serpent unveil his whole scheme to the woman in the garden?

114. How often does the serpent want the woman to partake of the fruit?

115. How many times does Jesus refute Satan's attempts?

116. What does Jesus use to defeat Satan's attempts each time?

117. Once Satan leaves Jesus, what does Luke add?

118. What will Satan do if we resist him?

119. What happens when there is no resistance to Satan?

120. Name some of the conscientious activities believers should employ to control themselves sexually.

121. What has been the indicator, which has lead to problems due to boredom?

122. What does singleness offer that is often difficult for married couples?

123. Given the adverse and pervasive effect of an ill-advised relationship, what is preferable?

124. What should singles and sexually frustrated spouses do?

125. While using self-induced forms of sexual relief, what should believers avoid?

126. Explain the caution concerning fantasy.

127. What is probably the most accurate rendering of "possessing one's own vessel"?

128. What did Jesus inform believers about bodily functions?

129. What did Jesus recommend concerning stumbling blocks (Matt. 18:8-9)?

130. What has the same purpose as plucking an eye, or severing a hand?

131. Does the Bible address forms of self-relief?

Jesus and Sexuality, Principles for All Believers

132. Once Dr. DavidSon saw the scribbling on the receipt, what did he realize?

133. Was he tempted?

134. Within hours what did he do?

135. What happened after midnight of the next day?

136. Once he could see that saying he had a family did not work, what did he try?

137. What did his two friends recommend?

138. After his experience with the woman at the credit union, whose life did Dr. DavidSon examine concerning sexual temptation?

139. What verse in the Bible says that Jesus was tempted in all ways, but without sinning?

140. What experience in the life of Jesus Christ provides spouses and singles with principles for overcoming sexual temptation?

141. What was Jesus physical condition when he arrived at the well in Samaria?

142. Who also came to the well?

143. What does the writer—John--inform the readers about in verse 8?

144. Who initiates the conversation?

145. What did the woman recognize about Jesus in verse 9?

146. What did Jesus offer in verse 10?

147. What type of question does the woman ask in verse 12?

148. What does the woman request in verse 15?

149. What does Jesus do in verse 16?

150. What does Jesus already know?

151. What does she perceive about Jesus in vs. 19?

152. Where did men typically meet available women (give at least one Biblical example)?

153. Was the woman at the well status conscientious?

154. Does anyone know what the woman expected when she asked for the water Jesus offered?

155. Is the woman thinking of spiritual matters when Jesus speaks of living water?

156. When Jesus asked her about her man, what was her reply?

157. Was she lying as far as she was concerned?

158. Why would she lie about there not being a man in her life?

159. Jesus responds that "in-fact" she has told what?

160. What has she never had with any man?

161. What does this imply about the relationships she has had?

162. How many relationships did Jesus reveal?

163. What does she finally recognize when Jesus tells her about these relationships?

164. What does she do once she is on the same spiritual plane as Jesus?

165. Given the evidence in this encounter, how was she viewing Jesus potentially?

166. Since Jesus knew her intentions, how did Jesus move right to the "heart" of the matter?

167. What would have been the implications for us if Jesus failed?

168. What principle did Jesus demonstrate when meeting persons of the opposite sex?

169. Unless they are already married, what is it virtually impossible to do if a believer is having sex with an unbeliever?

170. If two believers are having sexual relations, what do they need to do before they can consider themselves to be encouraging each other's spiritual development?

171. What must be held in higher regard than sexual or companionship desires?

172. What does a woman do to Jesus in Luke 7:37-48?

173. Did Simon perceive the woman's conduct as religious or a custom?

174. Did Jesus appreciate the woman's attention?

175. Did Jesus rebuke the woman?

176. What did Simon mean when he said the woman was a sinner?

177. What is Jesus more concerned about than companionship or sex?

178. What happens in John 12:1-8? Who envies her this time?

179. Matthew 4:1-11 reveals the temptation of Jesus in the wilderness. What is the first temptation?

180. Does Satan begin his temptations with his full intentions?

181. How does Satan challenge Jesus' ego?

182. What object does Jesus use in his response?

183. Does Jesus discuss whether He is the Son of God?

184. What does Satan use to tempt Jesus the second time?

185. What does Satan want Jesus to do to prove He is the Son of God?

186. What does Jesus know about His personal desire compared to His Father's desire?

187. Unsuccessful with the first two temptations what "deadly three" does Satan use to tempt Jesus?

188. What does Satan show Jesus?

189. What does Satan want Jesus to do?

190. When Satan showed and offered Jesus the kingdoms and their glory, what would the list include?

191. What else did Jesus probably see representing the glory of kingdoms?

192. How did Solomon respond to this aspect of glory?

193. How does Jesus respond to this final wilderness temptation?

When All Else Fails

194. Who in the Bible is mentioned most often concerning sexual improprieties?

195. What two offenses did he commit?

196. Do most counseling cases involve both of these offenses?

197. What did David think was going to happen when Nathan revealed David's sin?

198. What is the startling announcement Nathan makes when David confesses his sin?

199. What is so marvelous about God's love for us concerning the union of David and Bathsheba?

200. How do you know God's love is greater than the believer's own self-condemnation?

201. What can erase God's love for the believer? (Provide examples from Scripture)

202. While we are often afflicted, what does God do?

203. Can the believer expect to suffer the consequences of poor decisions and behavior?

204. What should believers take every step to do?

205. When a person is trapped in sin, what should the believer expect?

206. When the believer fails, what must the believer do?

207. What is the Apostle John's counsel concerning sins?

Counselor's Answer

208. Given the three types of eunuchs, which does the counselor think Jesus represents?

209. Why wouldn't Jesus be a eunuch from birth, or of men?

210. Why would Jesus be a eunuch for the kingdom of heaven's sake?

211. Given the impact and reality of sexuality on the human race, what is unimaginable concerning the Son of God?

212. According to the Counselor, why did Jesus resist any need for companionship and/or sexuality?

Christ-based Counseling (CBC)
The Process of Being Made Whole

The core of Christ-based Counseling (CBC) is the Process of Being Made Whole. This Process includes six constituents and strategic prayer for forty-five days. Regardless of the issue, it is important for the counselee to understand these factors.

The Counselee Must Be Born-Again (John 3:3-8): The foundation of Christ-based Counseling's effectiveness is in the faith dimension. Therefore, only persons who are believers can avail themselves to the therapeutic or healing process in Christ-based Counseling. Persons who do not know the Lord, but desire CBC must be evangelized first. Nevertheless, Jesus' discussion with Nicodemus in the referenced text makes the point clear. The counselee must be born again.

The Counselee Must Be Presented Balanced Biblical Insights (Matt. 4:5-7): God's Word, rightly divided is the therapy for right thinking. However, as shown in the referenced text, God's Word must be balanced and not some misapplied presentation of God's Word. This can be seen in the Devil's inappropriate use of Psalms 91. Christ-based Counseling relies on the appropriate use of God's Word, and understands the overarching principles of God's Word.

The Counselee Must Possess the Degree of Faith Needed (Mark 4:24): Beyond possessing faith unto salvation, counselees must believe that God will intervene in their personal circumstances. The referenced verse is preceded by verses 13-20 where Jesus explains the different types of hearers of God's Word: Wayside, Stony, Thorns & Thistles, and Good Ground. Each of these persons represents how "hearers" embrace God's Word. Regardless of the circumstances, Good Ground hearers <u>believe</u>. They believe that God "is" operating in their personal situation.

The Counselee Must Be Committed (Luke 21:1-4): Counselees must be thoroughly invested in the Process. The woman in the example gave "all" that she had. What a difference she represents compared to the typical person in our culture. Often people do not desire to make the investment of time and personal sacrifice. This Process requires complete commitment by the counselee as the woman shown in the referenced text.

The Counselee Must Do The Practical (Mark 8:1-3): Depending on the issue, counselees must do the practical or physical things. As shown in the referenced text, Jesus recognizes the need to feed the multitude, or they would faint. The practical matters must be satisfied, and these are usually understood. As an example, a person seeking a job must seek employment opportunities, and submit applications where applicable.

The Counselee Must Stay In The Process (John 15:3-9): Persons who encounter any issue must be willing to invest time in counseling, prayer, study, and application of God's Word. It is popular to look for the immediate answer and quick solution. However, the essence of a problem is that the answer may not result in an immediate resolution. Therefore, counselees must stay in the counseling process as scheduled. Also, they must be engaged in the greater fellowship of believers, and on-going development in Christ.

Forty-Five Days of Prayer

Important to the counseling process is the additional therapeutic dimension of strategic prayer. As opposed to generalized prayer, the term strategic is used to denote the specific focus of prayer. Remember, Christ-based Counseling works with both dimensions (i.e., the natural and spiritual). The Lord has empowered believers to impact the spiritual dimension.

Why Forty-five Days? As mentioned in the sixth constituent of the Process of Being Made Whole, issues faced by most counselees represent problems that will not be resolved in a short timeframe. Additionally, many believers do not have a daily and concentrated prayer regimen.

Most important life changes require a transition, which usually involves the combination of an established timeframe and a different behavioral pattern, focus, or practice.

Biblically, the number forty is used so often it is more than a mere coincident. Other significant numbers, which most of us hear about are three and seven. There are others not mentioned as significantly.

One must be cautious about the use of numbers. There is always the danger that one may be overcome by superstition and mysticism involving numbers. Praying for forty-five days has nothing to do with any kind of superstition.

Biblically, [after sin] it appears that it requires a timeframe of about forty earth days or years for the operation of angels to complete an assignment. The term, "earth days" are used for our (i.e., human) benefit. Angels are the purveyors of God's will. That is, they are the workers at God's command who cause results in the material universe. God uses the angels to create, change, or allow our circumstances. They work in the angelic dimension, but their results are manifested in the physical dimension. Clearly, God has connected our prayers to their operation. There are more than 250 references to angels in the Bible.

Since angels are not limited by time or space, they merely refer to days for our benefit (e.g., Dan. 10:13). Therefore, the events in Scripture involving "forty" often refer to the completion of a phase, process, or administration. If this is true, the principle should be witnessed at least three times in Scripture (Deuteronomy 17:6; Matthew 18:16). Examples are provided as follows:

Genesis 7:12: It rained forty days and forty nights (i.e., the Flood) before the renewal of the earth.

Numbers 13:25: Moses commissioned spies to assess the land for forty days. They returned before making their final decision concerning the Promised Land. When they were found to be unfaithful, they wandered for forty years.

Deuteronomy 10:10: Both times the tablets of the Ten Commandments required forty days to complete before being presented to the Hebrews.

I Kings 19:5-8: Prompted by two angels to eat, afterwards, Elijah fasts for forty days and nights before journeying to Mt. Horeb. There, he received transition instructions.

Ezekiel 4:6: God instructed the prophet to lie on his side for forty days as an object lesson to Judah representing the years of Judah's iniquity.

Daniel 10:13, 20: Bewildered about a vision, Daniel prays for understanding. The angel reveals that it took him twenty-one days to arrive, but the angel's mission was not concluded. He had to return and continue his battle with the prince of Persia--at least another 21 days.

Jonah 3:4: The prophet warned Nineveh that it had forty days before being overthrown. They repented and averted their doom.

The Old Testament is where the precedent is found for the significance of a timeframe covering at least forty days. More importantly, there are two extraordinary events in the life of Jesus involving forty-day periods. **First**, the gospels (Matthew 4:2; Mark 1:3; Luke 4:2) record Jesus' wilderness journey before initiating His earthly ministry. This period launching His earthly ministry was forty days and forty nights. Angels were on the scene ministering to Him (Matt. 4:11; Mark 1:13). **Secondly**, as an irrefutable demonstration of His resurrection, Jesus appeared and ministered for a period of forty days (Acts 1:3). Again, angels were on the scene as He departed earth (Acts 1:10-11).

It is noteworthy here that one of the important characteristics Jesus taught about prayer was persistency (Luke 11:5-8; Luke 18:1-8). Luke 18:1 provides the specific purpose for the instructions on prayer. Pointedly, He instructed that we must not loose heart (KJV) or give up (NIV). The Apostle Paul used terms such as "pray without ceasing" and "always praying" (Eph. 6:18; Col. 1:3; I Th. 5:17).

Recall the case where a boy was psychotic (Matt. 17:14-21), and the disciples could not cure him. Jesus rebuked the demon in the boy, and he was cured. The disciples wanted to know why they could not cure the boy. Jesus identified the problem: Their lack of faith demonstrated by the absence of prayer and fasting. Persistency in prayer is the evidence of faithfulness. Therefore, Jesus did not mean they did not pray at the moment of need. He meant, "This could only be done by persons with a discipline of prayer and fasting." The most challenging issues in life require a process of faith demonstrated by persistent prayer disciplines (i.e., prayer and fasting). Disciples/persons with these virtues need only to strategically focus on a specific need. Like Jesus, their angels are "on-the-ready" awaiting marching orders from the Lord (Matt. 18:10; 26:51-53). **NOTE:** Believers must not worship, or pray to angels.

Clearly, Jesus knew the reality of what happens in the angelic dimension when believers pray. The angels are on the move, but they are opposed. God has connected their success to our faith or persistence. Jesus says, "don't loose heart." We must keep praying on a specific issue.

Finally, Ephesians 6:10-20 discusses the opposition to believers' walk in Christ. Paul makes it clear that the overwhelming objective must be to defeat demonic operations in the angelic dimension. Once this is accomplished, the way is cleared for "results" in the physical or material dimension. Please notice that the weaponry is spiritual. The Christ-based Counseling focus is verses 16-18. These verses highlight faith, the Spirit or Word of God, and prayer as the primary weapons. Paul adds, "… and watching with all perseverance …" No doubt, God can resolve a matter in a day. However, the Biblical evidence is convincing that a process is required for matters requiring spiritual intervention.

Finally, the term, "forty years" is also noteworthy. "Forty years" is used more often than "forty days." Consider that with God and the angels, there is no difference between forty-days, and forty-years (Psalms 90:4; 2 Peter 3:8). When believers pray in a range of forty days--in God's will, they will see a discernable change. Remember, this affirms a process or practice in the angelic dimension. The issue may not be resolved, but there will be change. In addition, a person will be closer to the Lord's answer. Obviously, some matters of prayer will be with us a lifetime. Others are not long at all.

Test it! If you have an issue, follow the six-steps, and pray forty-five days. See if there is an affirmative "change." Remember, the number, "forty" is not magical. One is to keep praying until the mission is complete.

Who is the origin of the additional five days? As Paul would say, "this is not the Lord's command, but mine and I believe it is worthy. An additional five days cannot hurt." sbd

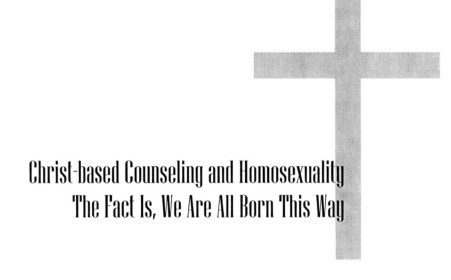

Christ-based Counseling and Homosexuality
The Fact Is, We Are All Born This Way

Christ-based Counseling Topics, Principles, and Practices

- The "issue" of homosexuality and the Church
- How Unfortunate
- How does a man lie with a woman?
- The creation factor
- The prevailing issue with Sodom and sodomites
- Our hypocrisy, the abomination factor
- No Biblical references prohibiting homosexuality!
- A closer look at the words homosexual and effeminate
- Any direct New Testament commands forbidding homosexuality?
- Homosexual claims concerning Jesus and His disciples
- The genetics disclosures
- How could there be a homosexual gene?
- Reaching the homosexual
- Recommended Christ Based Counseling Techniques

Due to the sexual nature of the topic, be advised that some of the material may be offensive.

The Christ-based Counseling (CBC) approach does not argue whether homosexuals were born "this" way. The CBC position is that there is substantive Biblical evidence to support their cry. However, CBC holds that genetic predisposition does not provide a Biblical waiver for homosexual behavior. The Biblical record demonstrates the opposite. Prohibited "orientations" of any nature are inexcusable and yet forgivable to those who "turn" from prohibited life preferences. Therefore, the CBC view is convinced that all sinners (i.e., all of us) are born "this" way.

The "Issue" of Homosexuality and the Church

A friend who shall remain nameless was greatly disturbed. Her pastor who was selected less than a few years ago initiated an on-going campaign of pro-homosexual instruction and related activities. Not merely activities involving God's love for sinners including homosexuals, but his objective was to demonstrate the Biblically appropriate nature of persons living such a lifestyle. He further belittled any opposition to his view. He referred to his seminary education as the advantage in understanding the homosexual issue.

During the last several years, I recall two families within one local church who were informed their sons were homosexual. The older son of the two was in his forties and his parents did not know about his lifestyle until they were informed that he was dying of AIDS. Needless to say, they were devastated by their discovery (i.e., both his homosexuality and dying). The younger fellow was in his teens when he and his mother relocated. It was not a surprise a year later when he announced he was "gay."

Both cases stated above revealed an interesting challenge to the faith of many believers. The parents of the older fellow began seriously considering whether their son was born homosexual. There was no question for the mother of the younger fellow. These families were members of "conservative" fellowships for more than thirty years. However, when they were personally confronted with the specter of homosexuality within their families, the rationalization and legitimization process began.

If there is a positive "conviction" element possessed by homosexuals, they do not have to be convinced about their lifestyle. Very few are in denial. Persons desiring to win homosexuals to Christ will not have to help them admit their acts. They are public, and they are proud.

How Unfortunate

Because God's Word is spiritually interpreted, it is easy to understand how something so obvious can be perceived so differently. On the surface it is unimaginable to think that persons confessing to be Christian could interpret homosexuality to be a viable "orientation."

What is the definitive characteristic of the homosexual? If it is that they are persons who copulate with persons of the same sex then the "Levitical" system (i.e., Law) is clear. Below you may note a series of legal violations where [if found guilty] one would face death:

> If {there is} a man who commits adultery with another man's wife, one who commits adultery with his friend's wife, the adulterer and the adulteress shall surely be put to death. If {there is} a man who lies with his father's wife, he has uncovered his father's nakedness; both of them shall surely be put to death, their bloodguiltiness is upon them. If {there is} a man who lies with his daughter-in-law, both of them shall surely be put to death; they have committed incest, their bloodguiltiness is upon them. If {there is} a man who lies with a male as those who lie with a woman, both of them have committed a detestable act; they shall surely be put to death. Their bloodguiltiness is upon them. If {there is} a man who marries a woman and her mother, it is immorality; both he and they shall be burned with fire, that there may be no immorality in your midst. If {there is} a man who lies with an animal, he shall surely be put to death; you shall also kill the animal. If {there is} a woman who approaches any animal to mate with it, you shall kill the woman and the animal; they shall surely be put to death. Their bloodguiltiness is upon them (Leviticus 2:10-16, NASB).

There are several "death warrant" violations listed above. A brief summary is provided:

1. Man with another man's wife.
2. Man who lies with his father's wife.
3. Man who lies with his daughter in-law.
4. Man who lies with a man as those who lie with a woman.
5. Man who marries a woman and her mother.
6. Man who lies with an animal.
7. Woman who approaches an animal to mate with it.

These codes, or laws are sexually-centered. That is, they all involve sexual acts or the potential of sexual acts. Please note the fourth. Man who lies with a man as those who lie with a woman.

Arguably, one could interpret this to mean that it is Biblically prohibited for a man to sleep with a man in the same bed. There are those persons who interpret the passage very strictly. One could consider men in dorms and barracks. Could these persons violate the Law as stated above? Fortunately a clear qualifier was provided. A man who lies with another man [as those who lie with a women].

How Does a Man Lie with a Woman?

Whatever the answer is to the question, a man is not to lie with another man similarly. If a man touches a woman when he lies with her, a man is not to touch a man the same way. This opens the door for the homosexual, as it were.

Generally, men do not "naturally" sodomize their women. Therefore, this provides an opportunity for the homosexual to declare, "we do not lie as men with women." It is a convenient argument, and it clearly illustrates the depth of desperation to rationalize a Biblical truth. However, the argument is destroyed when one considers something missing from the list.

Excluding incest, there is no violation of the law involving heterosexual sex. Please keep in mind the code above is not addressing the issue of marriage. The code is primarily concerned with inappropriate sexual acts. Therefore, one could not "appropriately" attempt to use the code as support for pre-marital or post-marital sex. Nevertheless, one could not consider marriage if the potential to violate any of the sexual prohibitions existed (e.g., woman marrying an animal).

Supporters of the homosexual view must strain to avoid such an overwhelming truth. There is not one Biblical prohibition against men and women being married who have the same faith. There are prohibitions against sexual activities involving people and animals, men with men, and men with relatives.

This is clear, and undeniable. No degree of rationalization can overcome such a truth. There is not one passage of Scripture that approves sexually intimate acts involving (1) People with animals (2) Men with men (3) Men with relatives.

Creation

Here the emphasis is on the creation of humanity It is an age-old argument against homosexuality that God created male and female, Adam and Eve (Gen. 1:26-27). There are those who have added, God created Adam and Eve not "Adam and Steve." So a great deal of effort will not be expended on the creation of male and female.

The real point of this section deals with the origin of man and blood. While most definitions of the word man find its origin in the dust, or ground (i.e., Adam) the Hebrew word for blood [dam] has the same origin. It is not the scope of this approach to deeply consider the etymological [word origins] significance of these words. However, it is important to note the close relationship between the two. This fact will be highlighted when we address the issue of Bible-based genetics.

The Prevailing Issue with Sodom and Sodomites

On the surface, it appears that anal intercourse between males is considered the "abomination." However, there is an issue as reprehensible to God as "sodomy." In fact, this problem is the basis for sexual debauchery, particularly the sin of homosexuality. Repeatedly, God compares Israel (i.e., His Old Testament, ordained people) to Sodom. However, His comparison was not related to the historic sexual acts of Sodom. God discloses something more egregious.

ISA 3:9 The expression of their faces bears witness against them. And they display their sin like Sodom; They do not {even} conceal {it.} Woe to them! For they have brought evil on themselves.

"They display their sin like Sodom, They do not {even} conceal {it.}." This is not an endorsement of dishonesty, (i.e., to "hint" that one should hide sins, usually people hide acts of sin naturally). The point is that they "glorified" their behavior. In contrast, history does not record the consistent pattern of any other group who so profoundly declare their sexual inclinations. No violators of God's principles declare and glorify their acts as the homosexual community. Can you imagine groups of adulterers, rapists, "beastialitists," "necrophiliacs," pedaphiles and others proudly extolling their sexual "orientation."

This spiritual and physical anarchy also found itself within the women of God's people. He declares their sin and His response.

Moreover, the \Lord\ said, "Because the daughters of Zion are proud, And walk with heads held high and seductive eyes, And go along with mincing steps, And tinkle the bangles on their feet,

Therefore, the Lord will afflict the scalp of the daughters of Zion with scabs, And the \Lord\ will make their foreheads bare. " In that day the Lord will take away the beauty of {their} anklets, headbands, crescent ornaments, dangling earrings, bracelets, veils, headdresses, ankle chains, sashes, perfume boxes, amulets, finger rings, nose rings, festal robes, outer tunics, cloaks, money purses, hand mirrors, undergarments, turbans, and veils. Now it will come about that instead of sweet perfume there will be putrefaction; Instead of a belt, a rope; Instead of well-set hair, a plucked-out scalp; Instead of fine clothes, a donning of sackcloth; And branding instead of beauty (Isaiah 3:16-24).

Their sin was pride and seduction, and His response was to strip away the source of their arrogance both physically and materially. This is the Biblical record of how God responded to the sins of His "own" people.

Spiritual "haughtiness" is the precursor of sin and particularly in the case of the homosexual.

Our Hypocrisy, the Abomination Factor

Let us be objective, frank, and truthful. There are inordinate attacks on the sin of homosexuality. There is not a sin that is more attractive to God than any other sin. Clearly, the result of sin, all sin, any sin is death (Ez. 18:4, Rom. 6:23, Gal. 3:10, Rev. 21:8). CBC recognizes that adultery, pre-marital and post-marital sex, and similar sexual issues are resident within the church exponentially more than homosexuality, and the Bible addresses issues of prohibited heterosexual sex more than any other sexual malady. However, homosexuals make a good target, and one that will not easily haunt the minister who seems to use the homosexual issue as a personal soapbox.

However, the leader or believer who makes adultery or extra marital sex his constant theme can expect major fellowship "slippage." Given the typical church of one-hundred members, the leader is assured that someone is involved in either adultery or other extra marital activities.

The point here is that homosexuality is not an issue plaguing the local church more than any other sexual sin. The emphasis on homosexuality makes other sexual acts more comfortable for those who participate in such acts. The truth is that all sexual sins are abominable to God. Most required the same penalty of immediate death.

Sadly, there are church leaders who have practiced adultery, and recommended adultery as opposed to homosexuality as if either or both were acceptable practices.

No Biblical References Prohibiting Homosexuality!

The Old Testament absolutely identifies homosexuality as prohibited behavior as shown. The New Testament specifically identifies homosexuality as fatalistic behavior. Paul, in his letter to the Corinthians (I Cor. 6:9) warns the Corinthians about the results of such activity. He warns, "Or do you not know that the unrighteous will not inherit the kingdom of God?" Paul continues, "Do not be deceived."

Note that Paul must add, "Do not be deceived ..." He details descriptively "persons" who will not be received in the kingdom of God. His list includes: fornicators, idolaters and homosexuals among others.

Paul also gives the same command to Timothy (I Tim. 1:10). Perhaps a person could claim to be a Christian who practices a homosexual lifestyle, but the person's confession would be inconsistent with New Testament principles. However, it depends on what the person means by being homosexual or the more popular term, "gay." What about the confessed homosexual person who abstains from sex, but maintains a position of living a homosexual life?

The King James Version uses the clauses, "abusers of themselves with mankind" (I Cor. 6:9), and "for them that defile themselves with mankind" (I Tim. 1:10). The KJV provides the ambiguity the homosexual community needs to argue, "there are no references to homosexuals in the New Testament."

A Closer Look at the Words Homosexual and Effeminate

Definitively (i.e., Biblically speaking), a homosexual is a "male" who participates in coitus with another male. While it is not the scope of this document to provide etymological detail, the Greek word for homosexual (KJV, "abusers of themselves with mankind") is arsenokoite (transliterated using English letters). Omitting Greek parts of speech (e.g., person, mood, tense, etc.) the word means, "males in bed." Note the "koite" ending of the word. This is strikingly similar to the English word, coitus. While coitus has its root in Latin, expert linguists know the common origins of Greek and Latin. Coitus is the "thrusting, rhythmic movement, and "ejaculative" culmination of the sexual act." Therefore, the New Testament's definition of homosexual is "males performing coitus with each other." A person who does not participate in such an act is not a homosexual from a New Testament perspective.

The person who would otherwise be homosexual, but manages to abstain from sex while maintaining a "gay" profile is probably effeminate. All homosexuals are not effeminate. The person who is "living in the closet," does not want anyone to discover his dark secret. This person could be the least expected of being homosexual because he does not have effeminate mannerisms.

Abstinence from "homo-sex" is a partial fix. The Lord desires to transform the whole person (2 Cor. 5:17, Gal. 6:5).

Paul's list of persons who will not be received in the kingdom of God, Paul includes the word effeminate. This is a different Greek word from the Greek word for homosexual. Paul who was filled with the Holy Spirit, and an expert of Old Testament principles recognized the perversion associated with demonstrating manners and behavior distinct from typical "gender" behavior (Deut. 22:5). Those who are familiar with Corinthians recognize that Paul directs his instructions to men. Husbands or men are to share Paul's instructions with the women (1 Corinthians 14:35). So his omission of women is not consenting to prohibited sexual behavior by women.

Nevertheless, the root meaning of the Greek word for effeminate (i.e., English transliteration, malakos) is soft. There are two other occurrences of this word in the New Testament. Jesus uses the word when he asks a rhetorical question about John the Baptist (Matt. 11:8, Luke 7:25). "But what did you go out to see? A man dressed in <u>soft</u> {clothing}? Behold, those who wear <u>soft</u> {clothing} are in kings' palaces." The answer to Jesus' question is a resounding, no! There was a major distinction between the way John dressed and persons in palaces. John, "had a garment of camel's hair, and a leather belt about his waist; and his food was locusts and wild honey"(Matt. 3:4, Mark 1:6). Persons in palaces dressed in gorgeous garments of silk, satin, wool, linen and other fine array (Gen. 41:42, 2 Chr. 9:4, Psa. 45:13, Ez. 16:13). Luke's account of Jesus' rhetorical question concerning John including an additional descriptive word is used, "... Behold, those who are <u>splendidly</u> clothed and live in luxury are {found} in royal palaces (Luke 7:25)." The KJV uses the clause, "gorgeously appareled."

The CBC view is that effeminate behavior or an effeminate persona is one that is distinct from the typical "gender pattern." The effeminate persona is so distinctive it is "stunning." Note the expression, "gender pattern." Gender patterns are defined here as, "manners, gestures, or behavior typically demonstrated by males or typically demonstrated by females." The effeminate's whole "gender pattern" is the opposite of the typical gender pattern. The effeminate male represents gender patterns of a female, and the effeminate female represents gender patterns of a male.

It is customary for persons using contemporary English to say that one has "softened" his position. This usually means a person was previously adamant about his position, but he or she is "moving away" from an adamant position, and is more likely to listen or negotiate. If we rely on the original meaning of the word for effeminate, it is equally applicable to men or women. A woman whose gender pattern is strikingly different from "female" gender patterns could be considered "effeminate." She has moved away or "softened" from gender patterns typically associated with females. The man who walks suggestively, or cross-dresses, or the woman suffering from "penis envy" are obvious examples of effeminate behavior. It is important not to be deceived by the etymology of the word feminine. Based on the principal meaning of the word, effeminate behavior can be demonstrated by males and females. Numerous nouns representing males and females are in the female gender in Greek. Most notably the word for church, ecclesia is female. However, both men and women represent the church.

Therefore, persons who abstain from "homo-sex," while maintaining an effeminate persona will not find an acceptable position in the New Testament.

Any Direct New Testament Commands Forbidding Homosexuality?

Ironically, homosexuals and their advocates can truthfully declare that the New Testament does not specifically forbid homosexuality. Paul does not give a "direct" command for Christians not to be homosexual. Paul leaves the choice to the reader. In I Corinthians 6:9, he simply describes those persons who will not be received into the kingdom of God. In I Timothy 1:9-10, he identifies the persons who are under the authority of the Law. His list includes: lawless, ungodly, unholy, murderers, homosexuals and others.

Paul merely reveals the expectations and conditions of the person who lives as a homosexual, and if the homosexual prefers to rationalize the truth, he has a "point." Albeit, the homosexual's point represents the epitome of rationalization and denial, and a point that will surely lead to eternal sorrow.

Homosexual Claims Concerning Jesus and His Disciples

The Bible discloses that Jesus was tempted in every way, but he did not sin (Hebrew 4:15). No doubt, homosexuality is a part of all temptations. As with all other sins, this makes Jesus the God who understands the plight of the homosexual. Yet, Jesus did not sin. This is a powerful image and hope for the homosexual who desires liberation and deliverance. However, accusations or perceptions that Jesus and His disciples were homosexuals are so desperate, and deplorable this writer merely responds with no response. No one should dignify such a mindless distortion of truth with an answer.

The Genetics Disclosures

Perhaps the most interesting disclosures are those which seem to indicate that homosexuals are born, "homosexual." There have been reports of a "gay" gene. This bolsters their claim that "homosexuals" are born homosexual. Therefore, "they assume" the right to be received as a Biblically acceptable "orientation." However, such research is evidence that something is seriously awry. Similar research is not being conducted to determine if there is a male or female gene. The ages have demonstrated by nature and the reproduction of mankind that maleness and femaleness are legitimate "genders." Both maleness and femaleness are forgone conclusions.

Nevertheless, it is not necessary for the Christian community to respond indignantly when homosexuals, their friends, family, and pro-homosexual "Christians" argue they are homosexual from birth.

The CBC position is that Biblically there is support for their claim. However, there is not one shred of Biblical support for the conclusions "homosexuals" and their supporters draw from such a claim.

How Could there Be a Homosexual Gene?

The Biblical perspective is that Adam's original sin affected his whole environment, existence and generations to come (Gen. 3:17-19). It is further understood that God revealed His principles for living (i.e., commandments, laws, directives), and the primary purpose for these principles was for man to identify objectionable behavior (Rom. 7:7).

The Biblical record further discloses that life of the flesh is in the blood (Lev. 17:11). Therefore, the conditions of sin are passed through blood lines of all creatures. Paul explains that as the result of Adam's disobedience, sin and its consequences passed from Adam to all humanity. Everyone is incriminated, "even" persons who do not violate principles similar to Adam's violation (Rom. 5:12-14). There are a number of Biblical references demonstrating that sin is through and from birth (Gen. 8:21, Job 15:16, Psa. 51:5, 58:3, John 3:6, Eph. 2:3).

Given these and other Biblical truths, it would not be startling if geneticists identified a "homosexual" gene. Likewise, it would not be startling if geneticists discovered other genes, which predisposed a person to adultery, murder, other crimes or acts of valor.

As indicated above, Biblically a homosexual "gene" is probable. However, the belief that discovery of a homosexual "gene" legitimizes homosexuality as Biblically acceptable is completely in error.

The person who practices "homo-sex," effeminate conduct, adultery, incest or other similar orientations is living an unrighteous life (I Cor. 6: 9-11). These persons cannot enter the kingdom of heaven unless they disavow such a lifestyle, and accept the life offered through Jesus Christ (I Cor. 6:18-19, I Jn. 1:18-19).

Reaching the Homosexual

Unfortunately, the homosexual's condition including pride, arrogance, rationalization, and sexual promiscuity represents a challenge that only a miracle can overcome. Fortunately, we believe in the Miracle Worker.

As with all sinners, only God can breakdown the walls of a rebellious spirit. Therefore, the first step is for the homosexual to recognize that his lifestyle is sinful. Once the homosexual views his lifestyle from God's perspective, he can "begin" the process of deliverance. This CBC basis will assist the homosexual with the first step.

Christ-based Counseling Techniques

Both, the Process of Being Made Whole, and CBC, Liberation and Deliverance Therapy are recommended.

College of Professional Christian Studies (Global)
Departments of Biblical Studies and Christ-based Counseling

COURSE: Process of Being Made Whole (6 constituents and 45 days of prayer)

Practicum Requirement:

Course Literature: CBC Study and Bible

Pre-requisites (if any):

Understanding the Course Design:

Students use the literature to respond to questions. Questions are in chronological order throughout the course. Questions preceded with bracket statements require Biblical, spiritual, or counseling insight and these questions test the student's ability to deduce, assimilate, and otherwise process a number of factors to answer the questions.

Completion requirements are as follows:

Sections: The course is divided into several sections of approximately 50 questions each. It is not necessary to complete all sections in one setting. However, you must complete a section before submitting your work. DO NOT submit a section that is partially complete.

1. What is the core of Christ-based Counseling?

2. How many constituents comprise the process?

3. What is the first step in the Process of Being Made Whole?

4. Where is the foundation of Christ-based Counseling's effectiveness?

5. Who are the only persons who can avail themselves to CBC?

6. What must persons do first, who do not know the Lord?

7. According to Jesus, what is necessary for any person who desires a therapy where faith is involved?

8. What is the second step in the Process of Being Made Whole?

9. What is the therapy for right thinking?

10. Read the referenced text (Matt. 4:5-7).

11. Satan wants Jesus to prove that He (Jesus) is the son of God. What does Satan use as the "authority" to convince Jesus that his (Satan's) request is legitimate? (Hint: Satan makes a reference to it in verse 6,"for it ...")

12. What does Jesus use as His "authority" responding to Satan's request?

13. What verse in Scripture does Satan attempt to misuse?

14. What does Christ-based Counseling rely on?

15. What is the third step in the Process that counselees must possess?

16. What must counselees believe in the third step?

17. Name the four different types of hearers?

18. Read Mark 4:13-20, which of the hearers has God's Word snatched before it can take root in the heart?

19. Which of the hearers receives God's Word, but "gives-up" upon experiencing difficulties as the result of obeying God's Word?

20. What are the characteristics of the Thorns & Thistles hearer?

21. Who believes in spite of the circumstances?

22. According to this step, the more a person believes and applies God's Word, the more...? (Complete the sentence/thinking)

23. Write the fourth step.

24. How much did the widow in the text give in life's value? (Hint: not monetary value)

25. What is ironic about our culture concerning lifestyle change?

26. What does the Process require?

27. What is the fifth step in the Process?

28. Read Mark 8:1-3. How long were the people with Jesus?

29. What physical necessity did Jesus recognize?

30. What is used as an example of completing a practical matter?

31. What is the final step in the Process?

32. Read John 15:3-9. What verb does Jesus repeat several times during the reading?

33. What will counselees be willing to do?

34. What makes most issues problematical?

35. Name two functions counselees must observe.

36. What additional therapeutic dimension is extremely important?

37. Are most problems resolved in a short timeframe?

38. Do many believers have a daily and concentrated prayer regimen?

39. What do most life changes require?

40. Name two factors necessary to reach a lifestyle change.

41. What number is used so often in the Bible that it is clearly more than a coincident?

42. What other numbers are seen often in the Bible?

43. What must believers be cautious about concerning numbers?

44. After sin, what is apparent concerning the timeframe of about forty days?

45. What is meant by the term, "Angels are purveyors of God's will?"

46. What specifically do angels accomplish?

47. Where do angels work?

48. What has God connected to their operation?

49. How many references to angels are in the Bible?

50. Why do angels refer to days in the Bible (e.g., Dan. 10:13)?

51. Events in the Bible involving "forty" refer to the completion of a _____, _____, or _____. (Fill in blanks)

52. If the principle concerning "forty" is true, how many times should it be shown in the Bible?

53. What happens in Genesis 7:12?

54. What happens in Numbers 13:25?

55. What happens in Deuteronomy 10:10?

56. What happens in I Kings 19:5-8?

57. What was the prophet instructed to do in Ezekiel 4:6?

58. How many days did it take the angel to arrive upon Daniel's request?

59. Was the angel's mission over when He arrived to Daniel?

60. How long do you think it would take for the angel to complete the mission? Why?

61. How long did Nineveh have to repent in Jonah 3:4?

62. Are there more than two or three references to the use of forty days in the Bible? (Shown in the questions above)

63. Where is the precedent found for the principle concerning forty days?

64. More importantly, give two examples in the New Testament where the forty-day principle is evident.

65. Who was on the scene in both cases?

66. What is one of the most important characteristics of prayer in Luke 11:5-8; and Luke18:1-8?

67. In Luke 11:5-8, what does the man desire from his neighbor?

68. Was his original request provided?

69. Given his neighbor's original response, how did the man respond?

70. Recall, what is Jesus' topic in Luke 11:5-8?

71. What is the primary characteristic Jesus teaches about prayer in verses 5-8?

72. Who are the two characters in Luke 18:1-8?

73. Concerning prayer, what is Jesus' specific objective for believers in verse 1?

74. How was the widow's initial request received by the judge?

75. What type of character did the judge possess?

76. How did the widow respond to the judge's initial response to her request?

77. Eventually, how does the judge respond to the widow's request?

78. What is the primary characteristic Jesus is teaching us by the parable of the woman before the unjust judge?

79. What two terms does Paul use concerning prayer?

80. Read Matthew 17:14-21. Who was ill?

81. What were the symptoms of the boy's illness?

82. Who tried to cure the boy?

83. Why were they unsuccessful?

84. Explain what Jesus meant by His explanation for the disciples inability to cure the boy?

85. What do the most challenging issues in life require?

86. What must be demonstrated, persistently?

87. When believers have a consistent prayer discipline, who is waiting for marching orders from the Lord?

88. Believers must not worship or pray to what beings?

89. What did Jesus know concerning the angelic dimension?

90. Angelic success is often connected to our _____ (fill in space).

91. Read Ephesians 6:10-20. What does Paul make clear?

92. Once the "overwhelming objective" is accomplished, what is cleared?

93. What type of weaponry does Paul address?

94. What are the focal verses in Ephesians Chapter 6 for PBMW?

95. What do verses 16-18 highlight?

96. What else does Paul add?

97. What can God do in a single day?

98. What is required for most matters requiring spiritual intervention?

99. What other term is also noteworthy? Concerning God and angels is there any difference between the two?

100. When believers pray in a range of forty days, what will they experience?

101. Will issues always be resolved in forty days? Explain. Where does the additional five days come from?

Preface

One of the most difficult conditions faced by a Christ-based Counselor is counseling persons who suffer with an addiction. Christian-based Counselors must possess an in- depth understanding of addiction from a Biblical perspective. A basic rule of thumb is that an addiction must be resolved before any other counseling concern can be addressed. That is, if the original counseling issue was marital, and the counselor discovers that one or both spouses suffer with an addiction, the addiction must be resolved first or addressed simultaneously. This is necessary because typically, addictions progressively dominate and control a person's life. This will be explained further in this counseling guide.

This guide is dedicated to believers who suffer with some form of addiction. Understandably, it is popular to offer specific programs and theories for specific addictions. Biblically, addictions have the same root cause, which will be discussed in detail. Obviously, there are differences in recommendations depending on the type of addiction being experienced. As an example, a person suffering with a substance related addiction might require medicinal support. However, a person suffering with an addiction unrelated to a substance does not require such support. Nevertheless, the root cause is the same regardless of the addiction.

Addiction is so pervasive that no one is immune. If we do not personally suffer with some form of addiction, most believers know persons who do. I am no different in this regard.

Yvette is a believer who admittedly has battled with substance abuse since she was eleven years old. She explains that she did not know what she was doing as a child. Her story is one of sexual abuse as a child, and a life of partying and progressive drug use. During this period she was raped, and exposed to a number of other abuses. When she became twenty-three, she received the Lord as her personal savior. She has continued to battle drug addiction. There have been times when she has been clean only to return to her addictive behavior. As of the writing of this document, Yvette has been clean for several years.

I have a brother Chuck, who is an alcoholic. He has battled addiction for more than twenty years. He tells the stories of where alcoholism has taken him. He has entered in-patient programs on a number of occasions, and he is yet to break the shackles of alcoholism.

It is noteworthy that whenever examples of addiction are discussed, it is usually substance related addictions. Obviously, the difficulty to overcome such addictions and the accompanying damage warrants such coverage. However, this guide does not view substance-related addictions as the most widely suffered or most damaging addictions.

Later in this guide, a description of addiction is provided. Based on the description, the most damaging, far reaching, and insidious addiction is sex related. The societal devastation related to our inability to overcome or control sexual addiction relates to every other social problem.

Sex addiction affects humanity in general. However, it is currently a national crisis of "Biblical" proportions. One cannot avoid the daily barrage of sexual innuendoes, reminders, overtones, and undertones. This is evident on television, radio, news papers, magazines, and the internet. A hideous and ominous slogan explains the condition, "sex sells."

Where the typical believer cannot relate to substance related addictions, the typical believer can relate to sex related indiscretions. Notice, how I referred to them as "indiscretions." This is a pleasant and deceptive label for the most devastating addiction known to humanity.

When the issue of sex is discussed as an addiction, the overwhelming majority of us enter the picture. Regardless of age, gender, or marital status, most believers are vulnerable.

This guide uses sexual addiction as the basis for in-depth evaluation of addiction, and programming to overcome addiction. The Christ-based model provides for applications of Biblical truth to contemporary circumstances.

After studying this guide, there can be no doubt that terms such as "mental arguing" and "addiction threshold" capture the addict's personal struggles completely.

Fortunately, God's Word has the answer to addiction, and this guide is dedicated to the Yvettes, Chucks, countless believers, and your's truly who need this Christ-based Counseling approach.

Counselees must understand that while the Biblical illustrations in this guide are found in the Old Testament, the Old Testament illustrations provide the characterization of Jesus. While Moses is known as the deliverer, Jesus is the liberator, "consummate." Jesus is the deliverer, "consummate." As God provided Moses under the old covenant, He provides Jesus under the new and better covenant (2 Cor. 3:2-11; Heb. 19:13-15).

The religious authorities despised Jesus during His earthly ministry. They saw Jesus as an impostor, and religious heretic worthy of death. Jesus admitted that these leaders searched the Scriptures. Jesus meant that they studied the Old Testament, and particularly the Books of Moses (Genesis, Exodus, Leviticus, Numbers, and Deuteronomy). Notice what Jesus declares about the Old Testament Scriptures:

> JOH 5:39 "You search the Scriptures, because you think that in them you have eternal life; and it is these [Scriptures] that bear witness of Me; [brackets mine]

Jesus is the Exodus story! Moreover, as seen in 2 Corinthians 3:2-11, and Hebrews 19:13-15, believers have a far greater covenant relationship with God than the Hebrews. How much more then is available to believers who are in Christ, Jesus? Believers in-Christ have all they need to overcome any addiction. Specifically, this is a viable program for the homosexually challenged, or person sexually bound or addicted.

Liberation and Deliverance Introduction

The most miraculous story of deliverance occurs in Exodus. The very meaning of the title involves liberation, deliverance, emancipation, and salvation. Given this nation's Christian-Judaic beginnings, both believers and non-believers are acquainted with the man known as the deliverer, Moses.

During December 2000, seven men escaped from a prison in the State of Texas. Eventually, six of the escapees were captured, and one terminated his life. The story of how these men were able to escape outraged residence throughout the state and across the nation. It is amazing and alarming when we are informed about the escape of a dangerous convict. Think of the bewilderment and horror when several convicts escape from a prison in daylight.

While amazing, such experiences pale in comparison to the miraculous and righteous escape recorded in Exodus. Imagine thousands of families with all they own, escaping from the grip of the most powerful empire on earth. Moreover, consider that they overcame centuries of bondage, dehumanization, and socialization without striking a blow, firing a shot, or assassinating a leader. Their sole involvement was their "cry" and preparation for liberation and deliverance (L&D).

Similar to the Bible as a whole, Exodus holds significant and relative meaning for anyone bound and afflicted by man, matter, or man's conditions. This certainly includes any addiction.

Addictions and Addictiveness
A Biblical Perspective
(Part I)

Description of Addiction and Addictiveness

As described in this guide, an addiction is reliance or dependence on a self-destructive behavior, which increases in destructive results while diminishing in pleasure, appreciation, and self-satisfaction. An addiction further affects a person holistically (socially, psychologically, physically, spiritually). Relatives, friends, co-workers, and others usually become aware or hurt by the addict's behavior. The Christ-based Counseling perspective is that an addiction is self-initiated and externally perpetuated. This description is explained later in detail. This program is primarily devoted to the necessary steps to overcome any addiction as described. There are several addictions that are detrimental to believers' ability to fulfill their call or purpose (e.g., prescribed and illegal drugs, sex, eating disorders, excessive exercise, and other similar behaviors). Clearly, some addictions are much more destructive than others. This does not condone any addiction as being more acceptable. However, denial represents such a sophisticated system of rationalization, it is important not to equate an eating disorder with an illicit drug addiction.

The word, habituated is synonymous with the word addiction and its cognates in this counseling guide. Biblically, the word ethos is most often translated, "custom." Customs are a major focus of the New Testament because they often became as important as God's Word among religious leaders (Acts 15:1, 16:21, 21:21). Likewise, habituated-behavior or an addiction has a similar affect on believers. Ethos is also translated, habit, in Hebrews 10:25 (KJV). Some believers made a habit of forsaking the assembly. Nevertheless, the term habituated-believer is used to denote an addiction.

Causes for Addiction and Addictiveness

There is long term research concerning the causes of addiction. Scientists are seeking a genetic cause for every illness known to humanity, and addiction is no different in this regard.

Biblically, believers already have an answer to the scientific quest to find a gene, which predisposes a person to an addiction. A close look at the Biblical record from a CBC perspective reveals an important fact. Sin IS a genetic issue. Sin is a core element of the human gene. However, it is not detectable by scientific instruments. It is a spiritually discerned product of blood (Romans 5:12).

SIN'S GENETIC COMPOSITION CAN ONLY BE DETECTED BY THE MICROSCOPE OF BIBLICAL TRUTH.

Countless believers who suffer with some form of addiction reveal that the first time they participated in the behavior, they chose to participate in spite of the obvious warnings.

Genetic Predisposition: As stated above, some people are more predisposed to certain addictions than other people. However, believers do not face any issue that is not common to man (I Cor. 10:13). Addiction is not new.

The Bible proclaims, "Then the Lord saw that the wickedness of man was great on the earth, and that every intent of the thoughts of his heart was only evil continually" (Gen. 6:5). This verse is the "Genesisial" basis for the description of addiction provided above. Addiction is internally or self initiated, and externally perpetuated. The Lord "saw" the wicked results of man. Moreover, these external results were from every intent of his heart. The key word in the verse is, "continually." The Hebrew word translated, "continually" is comprised of two words yom (day or daily), and kol (whole or all).

It is a matter of record that persons suffering with an addiction as described, possess the center of their world. The addict is the "gravity-core" of his world and those around him. The addict's priority for living becomes the addictive behavior. More specifically, the feeling, euphoria, or other perceived benefit is the goal. The addict will use, manipulate, lie, pander, and abuse anyone or anything to reach the goal.

Genesis 6:5 describes the innate (i.e., in-born), and corporate (i.e., all humanity) nature of addiction, and provides the descriptive term to explain any addiction's duration, "continually." Stated simply, a person actively feeds an addiction externally, by acting upon one's in-born desire. The result is always death [death of dignity, death of relationships, death of mental health, death of spiritual fellowship, and ultimately physical death] (James 1:6).

The addict began by making a choice to indulge the first time. The thinking and decision was made internally, the act was done externally. Thus the description, "self-initiated," and "externally perpetuated."

Some counselees suffering with an addiction disclose that they did not recognize what they were doing when they first began. [See the testimony of Yvette above]. However, this would be the minority, and not a majority of persons suffering with addictions. Moreover, those with protracted addictions [long term] usually claim there were times when they discontinued their behavior. However, they returned to their former behavior. Clearly, persons who returned to their addictive behavior made the choice to return. It is typical for addicts to report they considered the choice for a period before finally capitulating. Whether it is the first time or relapse, the decision was self initiated, and externally perpetuated.

DeGENEration from the Beginning: When Adam sinned, the degeneration process began immediately. Here it is important to restate a Biblical finding from Sex, Sexuality, and the Believer on a homosexual gene. How could there be a homosexual gene?

> The Biblical perspective is that Adam's original sin affected his whole environment, existence, and generations to come (Gen. 3:17-19). It is further understood that God revealed His principles for living

(i.e., commandments, laws, directives), and the primary purpose for these principles was for man to identify objectionable behavior (Rom. 7:7).

The Biblical record further discloses that life of the flesh is in the blood (Lev. 17:11). Therefore, the conditions of sin are passed through bloodlines of all creatures. Paul explains that as the result of Adam's disobedience, sin and its consequences passed from Adam to all humanity. Everyone is incriminated, "even" persons who do not violate principles similar to Adam's violation (Rom. 5:12-14). There are a number of Biblical references demonstrating that sin is through and from birth (Gen. 8:21, Job 15:16, Psa. 51:5, 58:3, John 3:6, Eph. 2:3).

Historically, when God reveals the wickedness of man in Gen. 6:5 as shown previously, the genetic nature of addiction was well established in the human blood stream. David pointedly reveals the genetic aspect of his sinful decision concerning Bathsheba:

> *PSA 51:4 Against Thee, Thee only, I have sinned, And done what is evil in Thy sight, So that Thou art justified when Thou dost speak, And blameless when Thou dost judge.*

> *PSA 51:5 ¶ Behold, I was brought forth in iniquity, And in sin my mother conceived me.*

David's confession in Psalms 51:4 is not followed by an effort to project blame on his parents in Psalms 51:5. He admits his sin personally in 51:4. Psalms 51:5 is simply a statement, which depicts the depth of his and [our] depravity. Both sin and the dynamics, which lead to addiction are the result of our genetic relationship to Adam. Believers need not wait on the research of the "biogenetic" community to discover that sin and thereby addiction is a genetic issue. A CBC description of what caused David to make such a devastating decision will be discussed later.

Comparison between Addictions and the Hebrew's (Pre Deliverance): Perhaps there are those who would view the plight of the Hebrews in Egypt as forced enslavement more than addiction.

Those with such a position would argue that the Hebrews were in Egypt in opposition to their will. Therefore, a major difference exists between their liberation and a person desiring to be liberated from a self-initiated and externally perpetuated addiction.

The concerns stated in the preceding argument may appear correct, but the evidence and Biblical truth demonstrates an excellent comparison between the Hebrews' condition and an addiction. There are several relative and important comparisons:

Benefits of Egypt (Survival): The Hebrews introduction into Egypt is recorded in the Book of Genesis. They entered Egypt to maintain their posterity. During the administration of Joseph, Israel's son, the Hebrews entered Egypt to survive, or they would have certainly died (Gen. 41:57-42:2). Upon arrival there, Joseph with the Pharaoh's approval secured the land of Goshen. This was the most fertile and prosperous land in the kingdom (Gen. 47:1-6).

Similarly, people become involved in addictive behavior because of the immediate and obvious benefit. Afterwards, the addictive qualities render the addict helpless. Effectively, the addiction commands a life of its own. It dictates and dominates the addict's life. The Hebrews did not intend to leave Egypt. Well beyond the period of famine, which lasted seven years the Hebrews remained in Egypt. Even after their liberation was secured, they were not crying for liberation from Egypt. They were crying for liberation from the conditions [hardships, forced labor] associated with their relationship, and not crying for liberation from Egypt per se.

Again, this is precisely the case with addictions. The underlying reality is often, the addict's cry is because of the results of the addiction, but not the addiction itself. Briefly stated, the Hebrews loved Egypt, but they despised the bondage. Before a believer can begin the journey to recovery, the believer must come to grips with the sin associated with such behavior. Treating the addiction is not addressing the root cause. The root cause must be addressed, or the person will continue to relapse.

Success in Egypt (Multiplying and success): The Biblical evidence reveals that they assimilated Egyptian culture (Gen. 47:27). Meanwhile, the Hebrews witnessed exponential growth and success. Most addictions give an impression of success, pleasure, satisfaction, and even euphoria in spite of the initial manifestations of problems.

Turn of Events (A new Pharaoh): However, during the course of time a transfer of power occurred. This happened after a number of generations. The Bible proclaims, a Pharaoh arose who did not know Joseph (Exo. 1:8). This does not mean that the Pharaoh did not know about Joseph, historically. It means that with the passage of time and generations, this Pharaoh did not hold the same level of regard for the Hebrews as held by his predecessors. Persons who are struggling with addictions do not experience the same levels of euphoria and satisfaction as experienced when they first began using.

They may or may not accept the reality of the destruction the addiction causes, but the evidence of the destructive effect of their addiction is experienced by those closest to the addict (e.g., spouses, parents, children, friends, employers, etc.). Unfortunately, the addictive quality of their behavior enslaves addicts, and addicts are under the authority of the addiction. Thus, a miraculous intervention is required to liberate and deliver the user from the addiction.

The Dynamics of Liberation (Part II)

Exodus provides the process of miraculous liberation and deliverance. The Hebrews had to be liberated from Egypt before they could be delivered to the Promised Land. Overcoming an addiction always involves two major categories. If an addict is liberated from addiction, but not delivered to a healthier pattern then returning to Egypt is inevitable.

Cry for Liberation

Well before Moses is called as the deliverer, God heard the cry of his people (Exo. 3:1-7). The "cry" is what moved God to act in behalf of the people. The term "cry" must be discussed and understood. The "cry" in the context of the experience of the Hebrews in Egypt was the result of the depth of their need, the continuous nature of their bondage, and their growing desperation. Therefore, the word cry depicts a deep-seated anguish over a long period under worsening conditions. God responded, "for I have heard the cry of my people." What God hears is the sincere and deep longing in the hearts of his people. What evidence is there of this deep longing? Clearly, the cry or prayers, which are heard by God involve tears, longevity, and consistent pleading (Luke 18:1-8).

Again, we learn from this experience a basic, and yet primary method an addicted person must employ. There must be a cry to the Lord for liberation. This request must be consistent [pray about the same thing], continuous [daily], and over a period of time.

L&D-1 The Habituated-Believer Must Pray Daily For Liberation From Addiction And Deliverance To A New Pattern/Source For Living

---

Recall, as stated above, the cry is because of the change of events.

God's Purpose

Another truth shown in the Biblical record is that God had a purpose for the liberation and deliverance of the Hebrews. The word is given to Moses, and Moses proclaims to Pharaoh to let God's people go. This liberation is not for the Hebrews. The liberation is for God. This is key to an addict's liberation. One is set free to serve the almighty God. They are set free as a demonstration of God's power in their lives. Moses constantly and consistently gives the reasons for their liberation as follows: Celebrate a feast (5:1), serve Me in the wilderness (7:16), serve Me (8:1), sacrifice to the Lord (8:8), serve Me (8:20), sacrifice to the Lord (8:29), serve Me (9:1), serve Me (9:13), and serve Me (10:3).

Another truth becomes absolutely clear about the origin of the bondage or addiction. Moreover, this truth is that for every godly purpose, there is the objective of our sin nature. Upon departing from Egypt, the Egyptians reconsidered their situation and declared, "What is this we have done, that we have let Israel go from serving us?" Exo. 14:5. Addiction never allows the addict to serve God. Yes, the addict may desire to serve God, but the addiction masters the addict. The addiction is preeminent. The addiction has priority over the family, the addict's on personal well being, and God.

L&D-2 Only God Can Completely Liberate Believers From Habituated-Behavior.

God Calls an Intercessor

It is important to recognize the call of Moses. Moses begins as an insider raised by the Egyptians. He experienced the very best that Egypt had to offer. Egypt was not merely a fledgling nation. Egypt was an empire with great cultural, political, and military influence throughout the ancient world. Many of its artifacts and achievement are still considered some of humanity's most significant achievements. God selected a deliverer who knew the condition because he lived among his brethren (Exo. 2:11). He witnessed the condition, but he did not live under such conditions. Now, this point is particularly important. Often, we believe that the best counselors are persons who have personal experience with the issues they counsel. That is, a person who has experienced addiction is more likely to be an effective counselor of persons suffering with addiction. Persons experiencing marital problems are more likely to be effective counselors of persons encountering marital difficulties. While there is validity to such reasoning, this is not the principle God uses in the case of the Hebrews in bondage. Yes, he certainly uses persons who have made glaring mistakes, as did Moses who murdered an Egyptian.

However, in terms of this specific case, God used Moses who clearly witnessed the depravity of the bondage, but Moses was not under such bondage when God called him.

Similarly and pointedly, Moses was a preview of Jesus. Jesus becomes an insider who experiences our dilemma, but he is an outsider in that he never succumbs to sin. This is what makes an outstanding counselor in the case of addiction. The addicted person needs someone who understands the condition. Someone who has experienced the condition directly or indirectly, but is an outsider who is not under the control or influence of the addiction. This person can proclaim before the world, and in behalf of an addict, "let my brother or sister go."

L&D-3 Habituated-Believers Must Have One or More Intercessors

God Declares the Time of Liberation

Another principle is that God's liberation is time sensitive. Clearly, a believer's addiction is not a surprise to God. Recall that God told Abraham that his posterity would be in bondage for four hundred years (Gen.15:13). Observe that God made a promise to Abraham. He promised him several things, but most notably that he would be a man of many generations and a chosen people (Gen. 12:2; 13:15-16). However, he also provides information so that Abraham would know that God's promises would not be without challenge. So, Abraham was informed about impending threats to God's promise (Gen. 15:13-14). When everything had been fulfilled that God deemed as needful, he places into motion the liberation and deliverance of the Hebrews. The Hebrews had a spiritual commission to fulfill, and part of that commission required their own homeland. A homeland would distinguish them as God's people. However, when times are fruitful and productive rarely are we focused on God's purpose for our lives. Obviously, the Hebrews were not going to depart Egypt to comply with God's commission if the prosperity they witnessed during Joseph's lifetime and thereafter continued.

It required the passage of time and changing circumstances to reach a level where the Hebrews would cry unto the Lord for liberty.

Here, the CBC, Prodigal Motivation comes into play. The Hebrews depraved condition had to outweigh the benefits experienced in Egypt. This is often referred to as "bottoming-out." However, "bottoming-out" is not the key in a Biblical based L&D program for believers suffering with an addiction. Judas bottomed-out, but Judas did not recover from his obsession with monetary gain. No doubt, he felt guilty and he cast the money away, but that was not the root cause of his problem. The betrayal of Jesus and collection of thirty pieces of silver did not relieve Judas. His natural desires dictated his decisions. Subsequently, he killed himself (Acts 1:16-18).

The addict chooses to begin addictive behavior, but God decides when to liberate the believer. Moreover, when God liberates us from our "Egypts," He does it so that we will never return.

L&D-4 Habituated-Believers Place Their Trust in God's Timing.

God Assaults the Benefactor of the Addiction

Another principle that must be understood by the counselor and counselee alike is that God will assault those persons, things, and systems that benefit from the bondage of His children. This is a Biblical fact. The Biblical record is without exception. Kingdoms, persons and any other entity, which benefit from oppressing God's people, will meet their demise. This is such a serious matter that even when God used other "peoples" to punish His own children, eventually God would destroy the nations He used to punish His own chosen people. It is a principal matter that an enemy of a believer is an enemy of God. Moreover, the enemies of God will be defeated.

L&D-5 God Will Break Anyone or Anything Supporting a Believer's Habituated Behavior

---

Relapse Amidst Recovery

Another important concept of this program is to recognize the principle of deception before deliverance, or relapse amidst recovery. Remember, before the Hebrews are liberated it requires a series of plagues and calamities, and these events do not lighten the bondage. Because of these events and the mere request to liberate the Hebrews, the oppression was increased (Exo 5:1-9).

Faith at this point and a faith-filled focus are imperative. The Hebrews were going to be liberated. God had proclaimed it. He did not call the Hebrews to remain in Egypt, and He did not call them to be enslaved to another god who in this case was the Pharaoh.

This is precisely the same principle, which any believer with an addiction can embrace. Notwithstanding what appears to be a worsening situation, God is going to deliver the believer. There is a work in the believer that is to be completed (Ph. 1:6).

Therefore, the addict and significant others who sincerely cry for recovery can expect deceptive events and activities during the recovery process.

Personal Liberation, Interdiction, and Duration

Regardless of the issue, we all want liberation immediately, or at a minimum we desire to see some hopeful signs. This underscores the importance of not choosing to sin, particularly the sin, which leads to an addiction [as defined in this document]. The truth is we only know that when God so decides, the addict will be liberated. Additionally, the addicted believer and those affected must trust the Lord in such matters. As with the Hebrews, God knows the time of liberation. Therefore, instructing believers on interdiction is imperative. How ironic it is that the term, "interdiction" denotes religious prohibition.

Precursor to Liberation: Psalms 51 is classically viewed as David's confession of his sin against God. David's prayer includes the keys to personal liberation. David, describes three focal points, in the first two verses:

> *PSA 51:1 (For the choir director. A Psalm of David, when Nathan the prophet came to him,) (after he had gone in to Bathsheba.) Be gracious to me, O God, according to Thy loving kindness; According to the greatness of Thy compassion blot out my transgressions.*

> *PSA 51:2 Wash me thoroughly from my iniquity, And cleanse me from my sin.*

> *PSA 51:3 For I know my transgressions, And my sin is ever before me.*

First, David admits a high-minded crime. The term transgression means a premeditated, arrogant, and bodacious violation. His decision to become involved with Bathsheba, and subsequently his plan to have her husband murdered was not by coincidence or serendipitous on either account. These were strategic sins. They required premeditation with appropriate timing, and follow-through.

This is the "addiction threshold." This is the period when the believer is considering the sin, its consequences, and mentally arguing to commit sin. Prior to his sin, there is no doubt that David considered God's commands concerning these issues. The believer must pierce a spiritual hedge to commit a transgression.

Recall, how God boasted about Job. And Satan replied that Job was protected by a hedge (Job 1:1-10), but the classic reference is found in Ecclesiastes. "He that digs a pit shall fall into it, and whoso breaketh a hedge, a serpent shall bite him" (Ecc. 10:8).

___

L&D-6 Never Pierce a Spiritual Hedge

___

David pierced the spiritual walls, reminders and prohibitions, and committed adultery. Subsequently, he murdered Bathsheba's husband. Afterward, Nathan the prophet told David the parable concerning a rich man who had taken the only lamb from a poor man. This allowed David to be an outsider who could judge the acts of the rich man in the parable. David was outraged by the acts of the rich man, and quickly judged the rich man in the story. Responding, Nathan identifies David as the man in the parable, and clearly restates what David thought prior to committing this heinous act.

> *2SA 12:7 ¶ Nathan then said to David, "You are the man! Thus says the Lord God of Israel, 'It is I who anointed you king over Israel and it is I who delivered you from the hand of Saul*

> *2SA 12:8 'I also gave you your master's house and your master's wives into your care, and I gave you the house of Israel and Judah; and if that had been too little, I would have added to you many more things like these!*

Nathan's statements to David are not new revelations. These are precisely the truths David considered just prior to his decision to send for Bathsheba. These are the thoughts that the Spirit brings to our attention when we are contemplating a transgression. There is an ironic comparison between Nathan's words to David, and Joseph's explanation to Potiphar's wife when she attempted to "addict" Joseph:

> *GEN 39:7 And it came about after these events that his master's wife looked with desire at Joseph, and she said, "Lie with me."*

> *GEN 39:8 But he refused and said to his master's wife, "Behold, with me here, my master does not concern himself with anything in the house, and he has put all*

that he owns in my charge.

GEN 39:9 "There is no one greater in this house than I, and he has withheld nothing from me except you, because you are his wife. How then could I do this great evil, and sin against God?"

GEN 39:10 And it came about as she spoke to Joseph day after day, that he did not listen to her to lie beside her, or be with her.

Genesis 39:7 reveals that Potiphar's wife desired to have sex with Joseph. Obviously, Joseph could not do anything else for her. He was merely a servant in her husband's household. Notice there is no evidence that she was not an attractive woman. Quite the contrary, Joseph's interdiction is both social and spiritual. First, he gives the social prohibition to such a decision. He considered the trust, honor, and authority Potiphar had given him. The only thing that Potiphar did not give Joseph was his wife. Secondly, there was the spiritual interdiction. Even if Potiphar had not honored Joseph in such a manner, Joseph recognized it would be sin against God almighty to have sex with Potiphar's wife.

During the addiction threshold, Joseph's thinking was clear, persuasive, and determined. Notice Gen. 39:10, Joseph never relents even under the day-to-day pressure she applied. Notice she spoke, but he did not listen to her. This does not mean he did not hear her. He did all that he could not to allow her pleadings to become rooted in his heart. Moreover, he did not allow himself to be with her. Joseph had to stay out of her presence.

L&D-7 Habituated-Believers Must Avoid Addicts Who Encourage or Influence Habituated-Behavior

This is spiritual wisdom. The believer must stay out of the presence of people, places, and things that represent the addiction threshold.

There can be no doubt that David had the same thoughts, and same truths to consider as Joseph did. The difference is that Joseph withstood the addiction threshold, but David proceeded.

Comparison Between Joseph and David (They have the same

thoughts, but make different decisions)
David's Addiction Threshold Failure | Joseph's Addiction Threshold Success

(2 Samuel 12:7-8)	(Genesis 39: 7-9)
I anointed you over Israel	My master does not concern himself with anything [with me here]
I delivered you from Saul	He put all he owns in my hand
I gave you your master's wives	There's no one greater in this house than I
I gave you Israel and Judah	He's withheld nothing from me
I would add more if that wasn't/isn't enough	[Joseph understood he could have more]
[David proceeds and sends for Bathsheba. 2 Sam 11:3-4]	[Joseph withstands, and stays out of the presence of Potiphar's wife Gen 39:10b.]

Both of these men where called and anointed by God. Both of these men loved God from their youth. Both of these men were heirs of faith and promise. Both were tempted in a similar matter. One of the men withstood, and the other collapsed. This stands as an example, and glaring evidence for every believer who encounters the addiction threshold.

L&D-8 Habituated-Believers Remember the Goodness of God in the Midst of the Threshold Battles

---

Continuing with Psalms 51:2, David does not simply desire to have his transgression blotted out, there is a deeper matter. Secondly, he must address the thing that caused him to trangress. He adds, "Wash me thoroughly from my iniquity, And cleanse me from my sin." Psalms 51:2.

Here, David addresses the thinking process within the addiction threshold. The Hebrew root for the word iniquity means to twist or contort. David twisted the truth, which led to the transgression. This is classic rationalization.

David had to rely on a visceral argument to defeat the great works of God in his life. He had to convince himself that taking another man's wife was warranted. The Bible specifically describes Bathsheba's husband as a Hittite. This fact had some significance in David's decision.

Hittites were people who occupied Canaan before the Hebrews returned from Egypt. The Hebrews were commanded to destroy the Hittites among others in the land. However, they allowed the Hittites to remain in the land (Exo. 23:23, 28). Generations later David becomes king, and the Hittites are well established in Israel. Clearly, Uriah was an excellent and dedicated officer, but David "marginalized" Uriah. Apparently, David used Uriah's ancestry [in-part] as irrational support for violating his family. The Scripture declares that God was not pleased (2 Sam. 11:27).

David's twisted and perverted thinking is at the very core of his decision to commit adultery. If God does not remove David's ability to twist the truth, justice, and morality, David knows he will repeat the same behavior endlessly.

L&D-9 Habituated-Believers Pray That God Will Straighten Their Twisted Thinking

---

How often do addicts speak of circumstances, which led to their behavior? This is particularly the case when we encounter difficult or unpleasant experiences. We desire to do something that will relieve our personal pain, even if it is only for a moment.

Again, Joseph is an excellent example of a person who did not use his circumstances as the purpose for sin.

When Potiphar's wife pleaded with Joseph each day, he could have reasoned that his brothers had betrayed him. Joseph could have acted contrary to the principles taught by his ancestors. After all was sold into slavery. He was subject to the whims of his master, or in this case, his master's wife. However, Joseph recognized God's presence in his life in spite of his circumstances. He had a grateful and thankful spirit in the midst of his unfortunate circumstances. He did not use iniquity or twisted thinking to consummate a sexual relationship with Potiphar's wife. He did not twist the truth to support his personal weakness or pleasure.

L&D-10 Habituated-Believers Must Not Use Their Circumstances as an Excuse to Trangress

---

Finally, David asked God to forgive him of his sin in general (Psalms 51:2).

Facing the Principal Enemy: A number of Christian counseling models concerning addiction refer to Satan's activity. This program does not credit Satan with personal decisions made by the typical addict. Notice David's prayer in Psalms 51. There is no mention of Satan as the perpetrator of his sin. David conquered many enemies during his lifetime. He defeated lions, bears, Goliath, and countless enemies of the Lord. However, David's greatest foe was his own nature. He rightfully cries out to the Lord, "blot out <u>my</u> transgressions…wash <u>my</u> iniquity…cleanse <u>my</u> sins. Notice the use of the personal possessive, "my."

L&D-11 Habituated-Believers Target Their Own Nature as the Principal Cause for Their Behavior

---

The memory factor: Another important aspect of addiction is the lingering or lasting effect of such behavior. Even after the believer is forgiven, and is liberated and delivered from the addictive habit there is often a lingering desire. Yes, the Lord forgives us, and he can remove the very desire for the addictive source. However, many persons who have suffered addiction will tell you that there is a lingering desire that arises on occasion. Moreover, for some, they are continually battling the grip of their addictive behavior. This is what caused David [in part] to say in Psalms 51:3, "my sins are ever before me."

He was forgiven, and there is no record of an endless sense of guilt. He continued with his life. Nevertheless, every time he witnessed an event, which occurred as a result of his personal decision, he was reminded of his sin.

L&D-12 The Residual Effect of a Transgression is That Subsequent Addiction Thresholds May Be Indefinite in Duration

---

Fortunately, the Lord is greater than our personal desires, and addictive behavior. Given the healing power of God and his intervention, we are able to succeed as Joseph succeeded. Thank God.

Understanding the Threshold: Meanwhile, the L&D process may take the remainder of a person's life. As with all counseling matters, the counselee or addict, and all affected persons desire a quick recovery.

Clearly, the addict's faith is imperative. The Hebrews required forty years to conclude a trip that should have taken days (Num. 14:33-34; 32:13). Sometimes our actions and personal resolve requires years instead of days or months.

Nevertheless, the Lord is primarily interested in one's soul. There can be no doubt that a number of objectives are involved when we are suffering with an addiction resulting from a sinful decision. God intends that we would overcome not only the sin, but that we would also develop resistance to the same or similar sin in the future. There must be substantial character development. Specifically, the addicted believer is to become more like Jesus Christ through the L&D process (Romans 5:1-5; Romans 8:28-29). Rightfully, we want our spouse, child, relative, or friend to return to addiction free living, but God's objective is more eternal in nature. He desires a person who is conformed to the image of His son. Conformation requires victories, successes and progress, but these treasures of life are not possible without disappointment, discouragement, and failure. If a person were to overcome an addiction, but ignore God's eternal purpose then such a recovery is not recovery at all.

Clearly, if a believer does not want to suffer with issues concerning the duration of the liberation process, then interdiction is the key. The believer must be successful within the addiction threshold.

L&D-13 The Ultimate Objective is That the Habituated-Believer Becomes Conformed to the Image of Jesus Christ

---

Dynamics of Deliverance (Part III)

The comparison between addiction and the Hebrews experience after they were liberated continues. Notice, they depart from Egypt on a given day, but the process of being liberated from Egypt required years (Gen. 15:13). Therefore, recovery from a Biblical perspective is completely based on the intervention of God. Yes, there is personal involvement as with all experiences related to the believer's relationship with the Lord.

However, the believer's personal involvement is the result of God's providence upon and around the believer. Often as a result of the circumstances, the believer willfully responds. The circumstances, which led to a will-full response and the response itself, are the result of God's authority.

Biblically, there is no such concept as a person self-correcting one's behavior with bootstraps. Factually, bootstrap mentality is a problem the Lord rebuffs continuously in Scripture (Gen. 15:7; 28:13-15). The addict and persons affected by the addict must understand that it is completely the power, purpose, and providence of God that saves, redeems, rescues, liberates and delivers believers. Certainly, a willing and obedient spirit is required. However, these virtues are the results of God's Word operating in the believer.

L&D-14 God is Solely Responsible for Believers' Deliverance

A Period of Praise

Once they witnessed the marvelous liberation by God, the Hebrews established a record of praise (Exodus 15:1-18). Their praises extolled the events surrounding God's final acts against Pharaoh. Early in the delivery process, liberated-believers should write and maintain as a historical record the events leading up to their liberation. It should include a period of celebration. Notice how the women led by Miriam follow the praise with a celebration. Afterwards, the Passover is instituted (Ex 12:11, 21, 43; Lev. 23:5). The very purpose of the Passover was to remember God's intervention in Egypt. This would be passed to every subsequent generation.

L&D-15 Liberated Believers Must Praise God for His Work of Liberation in Their Lives
---

:
Odious Memories

Unfortunately, the Hebrews lived in Egypt for hundreds of years. Once liberated, it was not long before the impact of a new life becomes the overwhelming threat. As time passed, the oppression of Egypt was forgotten, and the pleasures of Egypt became a cherished memory. It is not unusual for liberated believers to forget the sin and hardships associated with their addicted behavior. One would think that after four hundred years of oppression the Hebrews would not dare mention returning to Egypt. Nevertheless, they preferred to return. Likewise, believers who have been liberated from an addiction must remember the goodness and greatness of the God who liberated them. The God who liberates has a plan to deliver.

L&D-16 Liberated Believers Refute Any Pleasure of Their Habituated Behavior as a Deception, and Look to Ministry Support Opportunities
---

Negated Prayers

The celebration was barely over before the Hebrews began complaining about their new life. In addition, this was not merely a subtle complaint. Their complaint included an insult toward the almighty God who liberated them. It is one thing to ask, "what are we going to drink?" But it is clearly another thing to ask such a question and then conclude, "would that we had died by the hands of the Lord in Egypt…when we sat by the pots of meat, when we ate bread to the full" (Exo. 15:23-24; 16:2-3). This is an attitude with grave consequences. First, they were liberated from Egypt, but not delivered to the land of promise. God was not finished. Therefore, their complaining was premature. Their liberation from Egypt was only the beginnings of their experience with God as a liberator. Secondly, their attitude delayed their deliverance. Their attitude represented their faithlessness. Therefore, it virtually negated their prayers. If it had not been for God's covenant with Abraham, it is doubtful that they would have continued at all. Consequently, the unbelieving and complaining generation was not delivered to the Promised Land (Num. 26:64-65; Num. 32:12). Many believers suffer relapse because they were only liberated from their addiction. If a believer is only liberated, and does not continue the program then the believer can expect the obvious.

L&D-17 Liberated Believers Can Negate Their Own Prayers with Sarcasm and Impatience, and Postpone or Cancel Their Deliverance

---

L&D Programming for Believers Suffering Addictions

Based on the study of God's principles concerning Liberation and Deliverance (L&D), Christ-based Counseling supports the framework for a Biblical L&D program.

Program Activities

- Understanding Addiction, a Biblical Perspective: This section in the counseling guide should be discussed in detail. Counselors should use their creativity and wisdom in developing activities or simply discussing the Biblical perspective of addiction.
- Identifying medical support [if applicable]: If the addiction is substance abuse related, medical programs or support must be discussed. The counselor should determine how long the counselee will be in an L&D program during or after the appropriate medical attention.
- Targeting the Root Cause: A session devoted to understanding the root cause is imperative. This will help the counselee resist any tendency to project fault or blame on anyone else.

- Identifying L&D intercessors: Persons who will pray each day specifically for the counselee must be identified. These should be persons who can be trusted to stay on course. L&D prayers must be offered each day during the program.
- L&D prayer training: This training is for the intercessors. They need to know how important they are in the L&D process. It would be further support if they studied Exodus together with the counselee. A weekly prayer session with the prayer intercessors and counselee combined is recommended. This is best achieved in person at a mutually agreed place and time, but it can also be conducted on the phone or internet.
- Intercessor prayer training, believer: The counselee has to learn the type of prayer required as outlined in the counseling guide. This is not a devotional prayer. This is a cry to the Lord for L&D.
- L&D principles: The counselee needs to learn the principles of Liberation and Deliverance. These should be repeated every session, and they should be committed to memory to the degree possible.
- Threshold training: Counselors must discuss the "addiction threshold" in detail. The counselor should create training scenarios for the counselee to practice. The counselor is encouraged to use the counselee's experiences to create scenarios. Role-playing is an excellent method for training. Train the counselee to bring to memory God's goodness. Train the counselee to identify as a lie any notion that the addicted behavior is pleasurable, etc.
- L&D study (Exodus): The counselee should begin and complete a study of the Book of Exodus during the period. The study should be conducted each day. The study can be found at Christbasedcounseling.org in the School of Biblical Studies.
- Praise Activities: Any progress should be followed by a written praise, which is maintained in the counselee's folder.
- Exploring ministry opportunities (non-leadership): If they are not participating in a Christian related ministry, they should identify one. However, they should not be involved in the leadership of such a ministry during the L&D program.
- Familial support training: Close family members should be briefed concerning the program. Additionally, spouses must be trained on how to support the counselee during the L&D process. The counselee must be informed that the family members will not directly or indirectly support any habituated-behavior.

Program Duration

Depending on the availability of other supports, this program is designed to be anywhere from thirty days to one year. If in-patient detoxification is required and available, thirty days would represent a basic support program after detoxification. Nevertheless, the duration is up to the determination of the counselor of record.

Sessions

Sessions should be held a minimum of once weekly. However, other program constituents should be scheduled to occur daily.

Program Reports

Summary reports should be prepared by the counselor of record on a regular basis. The counselor should prepare a minimum of three reports. One report should be prepared for the initial record. One report should be prepared mid-way through the program. And one report should be prepared at the conclusion of the program. Notes should be taken each session as needed.

Terminating L&D

The program is terminated after the days established at the beginning of the program. The counselor should recommend additional days and activities if necessary. Remember, believers are always in constituent six of Christ-based Counseling. They remain in the process.

L&D
Assessment Guide

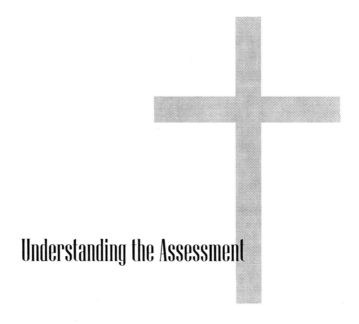

Understanding the Assessment

General: This assessment is designed to help the counselor evaluate the counselee's L&D program. The assessment should be conducted during the intake or first counseling sessions, or as soon as it is determined that an addiction is apparent.

Program Activity: A program activity is the component of the L&D program designed to help the counselee learn and apply an L&D principle.

Assessment Concept: The questions in the assessment are specifically related to the first 13 Liberation and Deliverance principles. Once the assessment is completed, the counselor can use the assessment to determine the presence or extent of the counselee's L&D activities. Once a determination is made, the counselor can assist the counselee by making the required arrangements to improve deficient L&D program activities.

Assessment administration: The assessment should be administered periodically to determine the strength of any L&D program activity. This is best administered on a consistent basis such as weekly, bi-weekly, etc.

Understanding the numeric rating: The ratings alone, where

applicable, do not measure how well a person is doing in a certain area. As an example, a person may participate in a behavior once per month. Generally, this is identified as being a good indicator of restraint. However, it does not mean that the practice is more acceptable than something occurring once a week. Committing adultery once per month is a better restraint than a person committing adultery every day. However, committing adultery monthly is much more devastating than a person who is addicted to working numerous hours every day. Therefore, counselors are advised to use discretion. Nevertheless, the higher a rating, the more established the L&D activity is in the counselee's life.

```
Counselee:(Last):_____
(First):_____(MI)____
Address:        _____   State:_____
Zip:_____
Phone:        _____        Assessment        Date:
_____

Briefly, describe the addiction:

Substance abuse (Drug, alcohol, other) _____ Risk taking _____ Fantasy_____
Sex related _____ Gambling _____ Spending _____ Excessive Exercise _____
Work _____ Other _____
```

Answer the following question to the best of your ability:

Directive L&D-1: Questions 1 through 4 assess the believer's prayer pattern. The counselee must pray daily, and specifically request liberation from addiction.

1. Do you pray?

   Yes [25]
   No [0] (if No go to 5)

2. How often do you take the time, and find a special place to pray?

   Other [1]
   Once monthly [1]

Few times a month [1]
Once weekly [1]
Twice weekly [5]
Three times weekly [10]
Four times weekly [15]
Five times weekly [20]
Everyday [25]

3. When you pray, do you ask the Lord to free you from addiction, or something similar?

   Yes [25]
   No [0] (if No go to 5)

4. When you pray, how often do you ask the Lord to free you from addiction, or something similar?

   Every time I pray [25]
   Often [20]
   Sometimes [10]
   Rarely [1]
   I don't bother, I have to overcome this myself [0]

TOTAL L&D-1 [_____]

Directive L&D-2: Question 5 assesses the believers prayer pattern. The counselee fully recognizes that God alone liberates habituated-believers.

5. In your opinion, who is most responsible to liberate you from addiction? 100 pts

TOTAL L&D-2 [_____]

Directive L&D-3: Questions 6 through 9 assess the believer's prayer pattern. The counselee must pray daily, and specifically request liberation from addiction.

6. Is anyone you know praying that you will be freed from addiction?

> Yes [25]
> No [0]

7. Are you sure these persons are praying for you to be freed from addiction?

> Yes [25]
> No [0] (if No go to 10)

8. How often are these other persons praying for you to be freed from addiction?

> Once monthly [1]
> Few times a month [1]
> Once weekly [1]
> Twice weekly [5]
> Three times weekly [10]
> Four times weekly [15]
> Five times weekly [20]
> Everyday [25]
> I am not sure [0]

9. How often do you pray with them to be freed from addiction?

> Everyday [25]
> Often [20]
> Sometimes [10]
> Rarely [5]
> We don't bother, I don't believe praying for something more than once [0]

L&D-3 TOTAL [_____]

Directive L&D-4: Questions 10 through 15 provide the counselor with general information about the length of the addiction, and the counselee's anxiousness to be liberated. The counselee must learn to trust God's timing. There's no rating for this section.

10. If you could do it, when would you like to be liberated from addiction?

☐ Today
☐ A week
☐ A month
☐ A year
☐ More than a year

11. If you participated in the addiction activity today, how much time has to pass before you would consider yourself free from the addiction?

☐ A day
☐ A week
☐ A month
☐ A year
☐ More than a year

12. How old were you when you first participated or exhibited the addictive behavior?

Age _____

13. How old are you today?

Age _____

14. Have you ever participated in a recovery program, or attempted yourself to overcome this addiction?

☐ Yes
☐ No

15. Have you ever relapsed?

☐ Yes
☐ No

Directive L&D–5: Questions 16-18 address the system, which supports the believer's addiction. The counselee must understand that the Lord will remove, terminate, or minimize anything or anyone supporting the counselee's addiction. There's no rating for this section.

16. Does anyone or anything "specifically" influence you to participate in this addicted behavior, or helps you participate?

    ☐ Yes
    ☐ No

17. Describe who or what specifically influences you to participate in the addicted behavior?

    ☐ Friend
    ☐ Relative
    ☐ Spouse
    ☐ Other (if Other, briefly explain)

    _____

    _____

    _____

    _____

18. When you feel the urge to participate in addictive behavior, do you ever try to convince yourself not to do it?

    ☐ Yes
    ☐ No (if No go to 20)

Directive L&D–6: Questions 19-22, assess the presence of the counselee's spiritual hedge, and the degree of restraint. Counselees must be trained to recognize and obey the spiritual hedge.

19. When you feel the urge to participate, how often do you try to convince yourself not to do it?

Every time [25]
Often [20]
Sometimes [10]
Rarely [5]
I don't bother, I simply do it [0]

20. How often do you participate in this addictive behavior?

Daily [0]
Weekly [1]
Bi Weekly [5]
Monthly [10]
Beyond monthly [25]

21. Once you make up your mind that you are going to participate in addictive behavior, which best describes how you do it?

Every time I do it, it is done away from loved ones [25]
Most of the time, secretly from loved ones [10]
Sometimes, secretly [5]
Everyone around me knows when / how I participate [1]
I don't care who knows, I do it whenever I'm ready or feel the urge [0]

22. Once you make up your mind to participate, how often do circumstances, or events occur which indicate that you should not participate in this addicted behavior?

☐ Every time I feel the urge
☐ Often
☐ Sometimes
☐ Rarely
☐ I just go do it

L&D-6 TOTAL [_____]

Directive L&D-7 Questions 23 assesses the believer's exposure to other persons who participate in the same behavior. This should be eliminated, or minimized.

23. How often are you around others who participate in the same addiction you face? (In a non-counseling situation)

> Daily [0]
> Weekly [10]
> Bi Weekly [20]
> Monthly [40]
> Beyond monthly [80]

L&D-7 TOTAL [_____]

Directive L&D-8: Question 24 assesses the believer's ability to recall God's goodness, and works in his/her life when they are in the "addiction threshold."

24. How often do you recall the goodness God has shown you and His love for you when you are thinking about participating in the addictive behavior?

> Every time [100]
> Often [50]
> Sometimes [25]
> Rarely [12]
> Never [0]

L&D-8 TOTAL [_____]

Directive L&D-9: Questions 25-26 assess whether the counselee is praying about the thinking pattern. Are they asking God to get to the root cause?

25. When you pray, do you ask God to give you the correct way to think about the addiction you are dealing with?

   Yes [50]
   No [0] (if No go to 27)

26. When you pray, how often do you ask God to correct the way you think about addiction?

   Every time [50]
   Often [30]
   Sometimes [10]
   Rarely [1]
   Never [0]

L&D-9 TOTAL [_____]

Directive L&D-10: Questions 27-30 assess the counselee's drive to rationalize the behavior with personal circumstances. The program activity should train the counselee not to rationalize addictive behavior with circumstances.

---

27. When you feel the urge to participate in this addictive behavior, do you ever think about your circumstances (such as how things are going in your life)?

   Yes [0]
   No [20] (if No go to 30)

28. When you feel the urge to participate in this addictive behavior, how often do you think about your circumstances (such as how things are going in your life)?

   Every time [1]
   Often [5]
   Sometimes [10]
   Rarely [15]
   Never [20]

29. Which are you most likely to think during periods when you consider participating in addictive behavior [concerning circumstances in your life]?

Generally, things are going very well [20]
Generally, things are well [15]
Generally, things are ok [10]
Generally, things are not well [5]
It does not really matter to me how things are going [25]

30. Given the following, which is most likely to convince you to participate in the addictive behavior

The feelings it gives me (any type of mental/emotional) perception [5]
It reduces the urge [10]
Gives me something to do [15]
I don't know [20]
A combination of the above [10]

L&D-10 TOTAL [_____]

Directive L&D-11: This assesses who or what the counselee identifies as the cause for the addiction. The answer must be self, or strikingly similar without other contributing factors.

31. If you could identify the number one factor that caused the addictive behavior what would it be? (If you have relapsed, then what caused the relapse)? 100.

L&D-11 TOTAL [_____]

L&D-12 is omitted

Directive L&D-13: Question 32, assesses the counselee's purpose for being liberated from addition. The answer must be to fulfill God's purpose, or something striking similar. If it is placed first assess 99, 2nd equals 66, 3rd equals 33 and if not at all 0.

32. Give three reasons why you desire to be relieved of this addiction (in order of importance)

    1.

    2.

    3.

L&D-13 TOTAL [_____]

Directive L&D-14: This question assesses the counselee's dependence on God to deliver him/her to a new pattern for living

33. Who do you think is solely responsible for "deliverance" to something constructive for you and those around you?

L&D-14 TOTAL [_____]

All other L&Ds omitted

TOTAL PROGRAM ASSESSMENT _____ /1100 = _____%

Assessment Scales:

	ACTIVITY ASSESSMENT	TOTAL PROGRAM ASSESSMENT
80-99	Good	Good
60-79	Fair	Fair
40-59	Marginal	Marginal
20-39	Critical	Critical
0-19	Non-existent	

```
┌──────────────────────────────────────────────────────────────┐
│ Counselee:(Last):_____                      │
│ (First):_____(MI)____                            │
│ Address:        _____    State:____ │
│ Zip:_____                                                    │
│ Phone:          _____    Assessment      Date:    │
│ _____                                    │
│                                                                │
│ Briefly describe the addiction:                               │
│                                                                │
│ Substance  abuse  (Drug,  alcohol,  other)_____  Risk  taking_____ │
│ Fantasy_____                                                  │
│ Sex related _____   Gambling_____ Spending____        │
│ Excessive Exercise_____   Work_____ Other____       │
└──────────────────────────────────────────────────────────────┘
```

Answer the following question to the best of your ability:

1. Do you pray?

    ☐ Yes
    ☐ No (if No go to 5)

2. How often do you take the time, and find a special place to pray?

    ☐ Other
    ☐ Once monthly
    ☐ Few times a month
    ☐ Once weekly
    ☐ Twice weekly
    ☐ Three times weekly
    ☐ Four times weekly
    ☐ Five times weekly
    ☐ Everyday

3. When you pray, do you ask the Lord to free you from addiction, or something similar?

    ☐ Yes
    ☐ No (if No go to 5)

4. When you pray, how often do you ask the Lord to free you from addiction, or something similar?

☐ Every time I pray
☐ Often
☐ Sometimes
☐ Rarely
☐ I don't bother, I have to overcome this myself

5. In your opinion, who is the most responsible to liberate you from the addiction?

6. Is anyone you know praying that you will be freed from addiction?

7. Are you sure these persons are praying for you to be freed from addiction?

☐ Yes
☐ No (if No go to 10.)

8. How often are these other persons praying for you to be freed from addiction?

☐ Once monthly
☐ Few times a month
☐ Once weekly
☐ Twice weekly
☐ Three times weekly
☐ Four times weekly
☐ Five times weekly
☐ Everyday
☐ I am not sure

9. How often do you pray with them to be freed from addiction?

    ☐ Everyday
    ☐ Often
    ☐ Sometimes
    ☐ Rarely
    ☐ We don't bother, I don't believe praying for something more than once

10. If you could do it, when would you like to be liberated from addiction?

    ☐ Today
    ☐ A week
    ☐ A month
    ☐ A year
    ☐ More than a year

11. If you participated in the addiction activity today, how much time has to pass before you would consider yourself free from the addiction?

    ☐ A day
    ☐ A week
    ☐ A month
    ☐ A year
    ☐ More than a year

12. How old were you when you first participated or exhibited the addictive behavior?

    Age _____

13. How old are you today?

    Age _____

14. Have you ever participated in a recovery program, or attempted yourself to overcome this addiction?

    ☐ Yes
    ☐ No

15. Have you ever relapsed?

    ☐ Yes
    ☐ No

16. Does anyone or anything "specifically" influence you to participate in this addicted behavior, or helps you participate?

    ☐ Yes
    ☐ No

17. Describe who or what specifically influences you to participate in the addicted behavior?

    ☐ Friend
    ☐ Relative
    ☐ Spouse
    ☐ Other (if Other, briefly explain)

_____

_____

_____

18. When you feel the urge to participate in addictive behavior, do you ever try to convince yourself not to do it?

    ☐ Yes
    ☐ No (if No go to 20)

19. When you feel the urge to participate, how often do you try to convince yourself not to do it?

    ☐ Every time
    ☐ Often
    ☐ Sometimes
    ☐ Rarely
    ☐ I don't bother, I simply do it

20. How often do you participate in this addictive behavior?

    ☐ Daily
    ☐ Weekly
    ☐ Bi Weekly
    ☐ Monthly
    ☐ Beyond monthly

21. Once you make up your mind that you are going to participate in addictive behavior, which best describes how you do it?

    ☐ Every time I do it, it is done away from loved ones
    ☐ Most of the time, secretly from loved ones
    ☐ Sometimes, secretly
    ☐ Everyone around me knows when and how I participate
    ☐ I don't care who knows, I do it whenever I'm ready or feel the urge

22. Once you make up your mind to participate, how often do circumstances, or events occur, which indicate that you should participate in this addicted behavior?

    ☐ Every time I feel the urge
    ☐ Often
    ☐ Sometimes
    ☐ Rarely
    ☐ I just go do it

23. How often are you around others who participate in the same addiction you face? (In a non-counseling situation)

☐ Daily
☐ Weekly
☐ Bi Weekly
☐ Monthly
☐ Beyond monthly

24. How often do you recall the goodness God has shown you and His love for you when you are thinking about participating in the addictive behavior?

☐ Every time
☐ Often
☐ Sometimes
☐ Rarely
☐ Never

25. When you pray, do you ask God to give you the correct way to think about the addiction you are dealing with?

☐ Yes
☐ No (if No go to 27)

26. When you pray, how often do you ask God to correct the way you think about addiction?

☐ Every time
☐ Often
☐ Sometimes
☐ Rarely
☐ Never

27. When you feel the urge to participate in this addictive behavior, do you ever think about your circumstances (such as how things are going in your life)?

☐ Yes
☐ No (if No go to 30)

28. When you feel the urge to participate in this addictive behavior, how often do you think about your circumstances (such as how things are going in your life)?

☐ Every time
☐ Often
☐ Sometimes
☐ Rarely
☐ Never

29. Which are you most likely to think during periods when you consider participating in addictive behavior [concerning circumstances in your life]?

☐ Generally, things are going very well
☐ Generally, things are well
☐ Generally, things are ok
☐ Generally, things are not well
☐ It does not really matter to me how things are going

30. Of the following, which is most likely to convince you to participate in the addictive behavior

☐ The feelings it gives me (any type of mental/emotional) perception
☐ It reduces the urge
☐ Gives me something to do
☐ I don't know
☐ A combination of the above

31. If you could identify the number one factor that caused the addictive behavior what would it be? (If you have relapsed, then what caused the relapse)?

32. Give three reasons why you desire to be relieved of this addiction (in order of importance)

a.
b.
c.

33. Who do you think is solely responsible for "deliverance" to something constructive for you and those around you?

Liberation and Deliverance Follow-up
Christ-based Counseling

1. What is one of the most difficult counseling conditions faced by a Christ-based Counselor?

2. What is necessary if you are counseling on a matter other than addiction, and you discover that the counselee has an addiction?

3. Why is it possible to use the same approach to most addictions?

4. Is anyone immune to exhibiting some kind of addictive behavior?

5. Briefly explain what Yvette, and Chuck have in common?

6. In your opinion, which type of addiction receives the most attention

    a. substance abuse
    b. spending (buying)
    c. gambling
    d. sex
    e. work
    f. exercise
    g. other

7. In your opinion, which seems the most wide-spread?

8. What does the counseling guide state as the most devastating addiction?

9. Discuss whether you believe this is true, and give an example.

10. Briefly describe the seven constituents of Christ-based Counseling.

11. While Moses is known as the deliverer. What claims can we make about Jesus according to the counseling guide?

12. Is the Old Testament, Christ-based? (Please explain your answer, yes or no.)

13. Do believers have a better covenant relationship with God than the Hebrews? (Give supportive scripture)?

Introduction

14. What does Exodus mean?

15. What was the Hebrews sole involvement for their liberation and deliverance?

16. What is L&D?

17. Do you really believe that God has provided a solid basis for liberation and deliverance from addiction through the illustrations of his works in Exodus? (yes or no, please explain)

Addictions and Addictiveness, a Biblical Perspective

18. An addiction is a behavioral habit that can be discontinued at any time.

    ☐ True
    ☐ False

19. An addiction is a behavioral habit without any destructive impact.

    ☐ True
    ☐ False

20. An addiction increases in pleasure over time.

    ☐ True
    ☐ False

21. An addiction decreases in pleasure, but requires the same or more participation over time.

    ☐ True
    ☐ False

22. An addiction does not have impact on others.

    ☐ True
    ☐ False

23. An addiction is initiated by someone or something else other than the addicted person.

    ☐ True
    ☐ False

24. An addiction increases in destructive results, while diminishing in pleasure, appreciation, and self satisfaction.

    ☐ True
    ☐ False

25. As opposed to the term addict, what term is used to describe a believer with an addiction.

    ☐ True
    ☐ False

Causes for Addiction and Addictiveness

26. What are scientists seeking as a cause for addiction?

27. Do believers have an answer to the scientific quest to find a gene, which predisposes a person to an addiction? If so, please briefly explain.

28. Using substance abuse as an example, is this a new problem to mankind? (Use a scripture reference that explains your position)

29. In Genesis 6:5, what does it explain about the intent of mankind's heart?

30. What were the results of man's heart?

31. How often did man consider the intent of his heart?

32. What do "yom" and "kol" mean?

33. What becomes the "addict's" priority for living?

34. What will the "addict" do to reach the goal?

35. According to Gen. 6:5, describe where the root of addiction is?

36. According to Gen. 6;5, describe who is affected?

37. According to Gen. 6:5 how often is the effect apparent?

38. Find James 1:14 in your Bible. Who or what is the primary source of temptation?

39. When a person makes the choice to indulge in addictive behavior, who is responsible?

40. Provide an Old Testament reference and New Testament reference to support your answer to question 40.

41. Describe what is meant by "self-initiated and externally perpetuated"?

42. Gen. 3:17-19, who or what did Adam's sin affect?

43. What was the primary purpose for God's commandments and laws? Provide a Scriptural reference.

44. Where is the life of the flesh? Provide a Biblical reference.

45. According to Paul, what passed to all mankind as the result of Adam's disobedience?

46. Provide a few Biblical references proving that sin is passed to each person through and from birth?

47. In Psalms 51:4, who does David blame for his adulterous act with Bathsheba?

48. According to David where is the root or origin of such decisions on his behalf?

49. In Psalm 51:5 is David attempting to blame his parents or someone else for his actions?

50. Is David attempting to excuse his actions?

51. How does discussing the sin content of human blood help counselors and counselees to understand the origin of addiction?

52. What two entities does the guide compare as having similar experiences?

53. Why did the Hebrews enter Egypt?

54. Who decided where the Hebrews would live in Goshen?

55. Was there anything unique about Goshen? Explain.

56. Were there benefits for the Hebrews to live in Egypt?

57. Where the Hebrews crying to leave Egypt, or to be freed from the oppression of Egypt.

58. Do persons who are addicted participate because of the benefits of such an addiction?

59. Do persons who battle addiction desire to be freed because of the addiction itself, or the impact?

60. What must an addicted person come to grips with before lasting recovery is possible?

61. Where the Hebrews successful in Egypt?

62. Do most addictions give an impression of success?

63. When a Pharoah arose that did not know Joseph, what likely does this mean?

64. Do persons struggling with addictions sense the same levels of euphoria and satisfaction as when they first began such behavior?

65. When persons suffering with an addiction do not accept the destructive effect of such behavior, give examples of persons most likely to recognize the impact first?

66. Who or what is the authority in the addict's life?

67. What is required to liberate and deliver an addicted person?

The Dynamics of Liberation

68. What Book in the Bible provides the process of miraculous liberation and deliverance?

69. What are the two major categories required to overcome an addiction?

70. If a person with an addiction is liberated from the behavior, but not delivered to a more healthy pattern and practice, what is likely?

71. Did God hear the cry of the Hebrews before he called Moses?

72. What moved God to act in their behalf?

73. Give three characteristics describing the Hebrews cry?

74. Read Luke 18:1-8. Why does the woman in Jesus' parable continue to plead with the unjust judge?

75. What is the result of the woman's plea?

76. What is Jesus teaching us about our prayer/petitions before our just God?

77. So, what is necessary for the habituated-believer to be liberated?

78. What are the three characteristics of the request for liberation?

79. What is the first L&D principle?

80. Who had a purpose for the liberation and deliverance of the Hebrews?

81. Provide an example of at least two reasons why Pharaoh must release the Hebrews according to Moses?

82. What is the Biblical purpose to desire liberation from an addiction?

83. Is an addiction designed to allow the believer to serve God?

84. What does the addiction have authority over?

85. What does L&D-2 state?

86. Was Moses raised with the benefits of Egypt?

87. Egypt was a weak nation.

    ☐ True
    ☐ False

88. Egypt was a world empire.

    ☐ True
    ☐ False

89. Moses was a Hebrew himself.

    ☐ True
    ☐ False

90. Moses witnessed the oppression of the Hebrews, and he also was oppressed.

☐ True
☐ False

91. Moses lived in the household of the Pharoah.

☐ True
☐ False

92. The Lord caused Moses to rebel against Egypt with military power.

☐ True
☐ False

93. Moses was a preview of whom?

☐ True
☐ False

94. Explain how Jesus is an insider and outsider to believer's experience.

95. Concerning relationship to the habituated-believer's condition, what does the believer need?

96. Explain L&D-3

97. Is a believer's addiction or relapse a surprise to God?

98. Years before the bondage of the Hebrews, what did God tell Abraham?

99. Did God make a promise to Abraham?

100. Briefly explain the promise concerning Abraham's offspring.

101. Was God's promise to Abraham without challenges?

102. Why did the Hebrews need their own homeland?

103. What is likely to be our response to God when times are good?

104. What was required to motivate the Hebrews to cry unto the Lord?

105. Is "bottoming-out" a key in a Biblical based L&D program?

106. Who serves as an example to demonstrate that simply "bottoming-out" may be completely meaningless?

107. Who chooses when to begin addictive behavior?

108. Given that the habituated-believer is crying to the Lord for liberation daily, who decides when to liberate the believer?

109. Explain L&D-4

110. Why wouldn't you want to be a person who contributes to the addiction of a believer?

111. Eventually, what will happen to kingdoms, persons, and other entities, which benefit from addicting a habituated-believer?

112. Explain L&D-5

113. What did God unleash on Pharaoh to convince him to release God's people?

114. When he learned of God's desire to liberate the Hebrews, how did the Pharaoh respond toward the Hebrews?

115. Is it true, Biblically, that when a person desires to be liberated, conditions could become worse before liberation is attained?

116. In spite of their worsening circumstances, what must the habituated-believer trust that God is going to do?

117. What promise can the habituated-believer cling to which proves that he/she will complete his/her work for the Lord? Provide the Biblical reference.

118. How soon do habituated-believers desire to be liberated?

119. Why is it so important not to commit a sin, which leads to an addiction?

120. What does "interdiction" mean as described in this guide?

121. Who provides an excellent example of keys to personal liberation?

122. What does David admit first in Psalms 51:1?

123. What is a transgression?

124. Explain the "addiction threshold."

125. Did David consider God's commands concerning adultery before he committed adultery?

126. What must be pierced to commit a transgression?

127. When God boasted on Job, what did Satan say was protecting Job?

128. What does Ecc. 10:8 warn about breaking a hedge?

129. What does L&D-6 state?

130. Read 2 Sam. 11:26-27. When David committed adultery with Bathsheba, and had her husband murdered, did he continue to have sex with her?

131. Did David think that he covered his sin?

132. Who was the prophet that revealed David's sin?

133. Give an example of the things God did for David that should have prevented him from losing in the addiction threshold, concerning Bathsheba.

134. Are Nathan's statements about what God has done for David new revelations?

135. What would lead you to believe that David had these thoughts before he committed the sin?

136. Who attempted to get Joseph to participate in a sin, which would lead to an addiction?

137. What did this person want Joseph to do?

138. What's Joseph's social interdiction to accepting the offer?

139. What's Joseph's spiritual interdiction to accepting the offer?

140. How often was Joseph pressured to indulge himself sexually?

141. Did Joseph listen to the sexual offers?

142. Did Joseph hear the sexual offers?

143. What did Joseph do to win the daily addiction threshold battles?

144. What does L&D-7 state?

145. What is the difference between Joseph and David within the addiction threshold?

146. What specifically does Joseph recall to memory when he was in the midst of the threshold?

147. David was called and anointed.

    ☐ True
    ☐ False

148. Joseph was not called and anointed.

    ☐ True
    ☐ False

149. Only one of them was an heir of faith and promise.

    ☐ True
    ☐ False

150. Both of them were tempted sexually.

    ☐ True
    ☐ False

151. Both of them failed in the addiction threshold.

    ☐ True
    ☐ False

152. What do believers remember in the midst of the threshold battles?

153. After his transgressions are blotted out, what else does David desire?

154. What does iniquity mean?

155. What did David have to rely on to defeat the great works of God in his life?

156. Did David have to convince himself that taking another man's wife was somehow warranted?

157. When David inquired about Bathsheba, what did the writer specify about Bathsheba's husband?

158. Who were the Hittites?

159. Is Uriah's nationality an additional reason for David to draw closer to committing adultery with his wife?

160. What will happen if God does not "wash" David's ability to twist or rationalize the truth?

161. Briefly state L&D-9?

162. Do habituated-believers often think about their circumstances to justify their behavior?

163. Who is an example of a person who resisted and won the "threshold battles" each day?

164. What circumstances could this person used to support accepting the offers of Potiphar's wife?

165. What or who did he recognize in his life in spite of his circumstances?

166. What kind of attitude did he have in the midst of his unfortunate circumstances?

167. Explain L&D-10

168. After asking God to blot out his transgressions and wash his iniquities, what thirdly does David ask?

169. Who is not credited with the decisions made by the habituated believer in the addiction threshold?

170. Does David mention Satan as the person responsible for his transgressions?

171. Does David mention Satan as the person responsible for his iniquity?

172. Does David mention Satan as the person responsible for his sins?

173. Who or what was David's greatest foe?

174. Read Romans Chapter 7. Given David's confessions in Psalms 51 and Paul's writings in Romans Chapter 7, who or what must the habituated learn to overcome?

175. The key to overcoming the principal enemy for a habituated-believer is to ask the Lord daily to BWC. What is BWC?

176. Briefly explain L&D-11.

177. What is often the result of an addiction after the habituated-believer has overcome the practice or behavior?

178. What do habituated-believers often express after they have overcome the habituated practice or behavior?

179. What did David say, or how did he refer to this condition?

180. Did David make his statement out of guilt, or the constant reminder of results he caused?

181. Explain L&D-12

182. Who serves as an example that we can be victorious in each threshold battle whether before an addiction is conceived or afterward?

183. Who enables such an ability within us?

184. How long can the L&D process take?

185. What would you state to a habituated-believer's question about how long it will take to overcome the addiction?

186. What Biblical example would you give?

187. What is God's primary interest?

188. What does God intend?

189. What or who is the believer to become more like through the L&D process?

190. What is often a spouse, child, or relative's desire for the habituated-believer?

191. What is God's desire?

192. What does conformation require?

193. What is the irony of a person who recovers, but ignores God's eternal purpose?

194. What is key if a believer does not desire to suffer with issues such as the duration of the liberation process?

195. Briefly discuss L&D-13.

Dynamics of Deliverance

196. The Hebrews were liberated from Egypt on a given day. Did it take a day to liberate the Hebrews? Explain.

197. Who must intervene for a habituated-believer to be liberated?

198. Is there personal involvement by the believer?

199. Who motivates the believer's response or participation?

200. What often causes the believer to respond willfully?

201. Can a habituated-believer use the bootstrap mentality?

202. Who has the power and provides the way for the habituated believer to be delivered?

203. Briefly discuss L&D 14.

204. Once God liberated the Hebrews, what was one of their first acts?

205. When a habituated-believer is liberated, what exercise should the believer practice?

206. What else did the Hebrews institute?

207. Briefly explain L&D 15

208. Once liberated, what becomes the overwhelming threat?

209. As time passes, what might a habituated-believer forget, and what becomes a cherished memory?

210. What must believers remember who have been liberated from addictive behavior?

211. Briefly explain L&D-16

212. What was the object of the Hebrews' complaint initially?

213. .Was their complaint subtle? Explain.

214. What did their attitude do?

215. What caused God to continue with the Hebrews?

216. What happened to the unbelieving and complaining generation?

217. Why do many habituated-believers suffer relapse?

218. Briefly explain L&D -17.

219. The following is a series of counseling scenarios. Outline an
     L&D program for each one.

    You are counseling a couple, and the husband is constantly
promiscuous in spite of his personal desire to do otherwise. Outline an
L&D program for him.

    You are counseling a couple, and the wife has a spending habit
that she cannot control. Outline an L&D program for her.

    You are counseling a young-adult who has a substance abuse
addiction. Outline an L&D program for her.

Christ-based Counseling, Biblical Basis (Exodus)

Exodus 1:1-10

What was the size of Jacob's family when they entered Egypt?

Had Joseph died, along with his brothers and all of their generation?

Which scripture indicates that the offspring of grew and filled the land?

What became the concern of the new king of Egypt?

Exodus 1:10-20

What did the Egyptians do to control the Hebrews?

What was the result of afflicting the Hebrews?

What did the king ask the Hebrew midwives to do?

How did the Hebrew midwives respond to the Egyptian king's requests?

Did the Hebrew people continue to grow in spite of the Egyptian king's efforts?

What did God do for the midwives because of their fear for him?

Since the midwives would not obey the king, what did he ask all his people to do?

Exodus 2:1-10

What tribe did the man and woman who were married belong too?

What did the woman do with her son?

Who watched the baby at a distance?

Who was bathing in the Nile only to observe the child floating in the river?

When Pharaoh's daughter saw the child, who arrived on the scene and said she would locate a nurse?

Who did the girl call to nurse the baby?

Whose son did the child become?

What was the child's name, and what does his name mean?

Exodus 2:11-20

What did Moses see as he looked on the hard labors of his brethren?

What did Moses do to the Egyptian?

When Moses went out the next day, what did he say to the two Hebrews who were fighting?

How did one of the Hebrews respond to Moses?

Why did Moses become afraid?

What happened when Pharaoh heard about Moses behavior?

How did Moses respond to the Pharaoh's efforts against him?

Who had seven daughters?

Who stood up and helped the priest's daughters?

When the girls returned to soon, who asked why they had returned so quickly?

Exodus 3:1-10

Where was Moses when the angel of the Lord appeared to him?

What did Moses behold there?

Who called Moses' name?

Why was Moses told to remove his sandals?

What was the 4-part description God gave about Himself?

What did Moses do when he heard this description?

What did God he has surely seen?

AND what did God say that he had come down to do?

Where would the Hebrews be relocated?

Who was God going to send Moses to deliver?

Exodus 3:11-22

What was Moses response to God concerning God's command to go to Pharaoh?

How did God assure Moses?

What did Moses say the Hebrews would ask him about the God who sent them?

And what was God's reply?

Who was Moses to gather together first?

Did God know what the Pharaoh's response would be?

What did God say He would do to convince Pharaoh?

Was God going to deliver the Hebrews without any possessions?

Exodus 4:1-10

How were two miracles Moses would use to prove that God sent him, if the Hebrews did not believe him?

What was Moses to do if they still did not believer him?

What problem did Moses see about himself?

Exodus 4:11-20

What was God's response to Moses' concern about himself?

What in the verses indicates that God became annoyed with Moses attitude?

When Moses returned to Jethro, what did Moses request?

What did God explain to Moses so that Moses would not fear for his life?

Who did Moses take with him to Egypt?

Exodus 4:21-30

Who did God want to perform all of the wonders before Pharaoh?

Who hardened Pharaoh's heart so that Pharaoh would not let the people go?

What was God's purpose for liberating and delivering His people?

On their way to Egypt, was God going to kill Moses?

Who circumcised Moses' son?

Did Moses speak to the elders first?

Did the people believe Moses?

Exodus 5:1-10

After telling the people about God's plan, who did Moses and Aaron approach?

What was the response to Moses and Aaron's demand?

What did Moses and Aaron give as the purpose for letting God's people go?

What was the Pharaoh more concerned about?

How did the Pharaoh increase the Hebrew's burden?

Exodus 5:11-23

Who was beaten for not doing the same or more with less?

What was their appeal to Pharaoh?

What was Pharaoh's reply to them?

Why were the Hebrews displeased with Moses and Aaron?

Why did Moses question to God?

Exodus 6:1-10

What did God say to Moses to remind Moses who God is?

Give at least two reasons in the text why God would deliver the Hebrews.

What promise did God make concerning his relationship with the Hebrews once they were freed?

When Moses reemphasized God's word to the people, what was their response?

Exodus 6:11-30

Was Moses concerned that the people would not listen to him?

Was Moses confident that the Pharaoh would listen to him?

At this point in the text, why do you think an accounting of historical family members took place?

Exodus 7:1-10

Before Pharaoh, who is Moses going to be like?

What will the Egyptians know when God stretches his hand out on Egypt?

How old was Moses and Aaron?

What happened when Aaron threw down his staff?

Exodus 7:11-20

What did Pharaoh's sorcerers do, and how did Aaron's staff respond?

What is the first consequence of Pharaoh's stubbornness?

Exodus 7:21-25

How did the magicians respond?

Exodus 8:1-10

What was the second plague upon Egypt?

What did Pharaoh ask Moses and Aaron to do?

Pharaoh understood the purpose for letting God's people go. What purpose were God's people to fulfill according to Pharaoh?

Did Moses and Aaron agree?

Exodus 8:11-20

What did Moses do to convince God to remove the frogs?

When Pharaoh witnessed the dead frogs, how did he respond?

How did God respond to Pharaoh's stubbornness this time?

Could Pharaoh's magicians do the same thing that Aaron did?

What did the magicians confess to Pharaoh?

Did Pharaoh let God's people go?

Exodus 8:21-30

What was the next act God inflicted upon the Egyptians?

How did God distinguish his people from the Egyptians?

After the insects swarmed Egypt, how did the Pharaoh respond?

What did Pharaoh say the Hebrews were to do when he freed them?

Did Moses proceed to ask God to take away the insects?

After God removed the plague, how did Pharaoh respond?

Exodus 9:1-10

What did God unleash upon the land?

Who quickly called Moses and Aaron?

How did Moses respond?

Who hardened Pharaoh's heart?

Exodus 10:21-29

What happened when Moses stretched his hands toward the sky?

When Pharaoh called to Moses, what did the Pharaoh say?

What did Moses insist?

How did Pharaoh respond?

How did Pharaoh threaten Moses?

How did Moses respond?

Exodus 11

Prior to the final plague, what did the Lord tell Moses to ask the people to do?

What in verse 3 indicates that the Egyptians gave the silver and gold to the Hebrews?

What did Moses tell the people the Lord would do about midnight?

How would the Hebrews be affected by what God was going to do to the Egyptians?

Exodus 12

How were the people to be dressed when they ate this final meal?

How were the people to eat this meal?

☐ Slowly
☐ Didn't Matter
☐ Quickly

What did the Lord call this meal?

Why did he call it this name?

Where they to celebrate this date throughout all generations?

What kind of bread were the Hebrews to eat during the first seven days of the New Year?

What happened to a person who ate leavened bread?

What were the Hebrews to continue doing once they entered their own land?

What were the Hebrews to tell their children whenever the children asked about the meaning of the pass over celebration?

What did the Lord do at midnight?

Other than the Hebrews was there any home in Egypt where there was not someone dead?

Exodus 12:31-40

What did the Pharaoh tell Moses and Aaron to do?

Did the Hebrews have any possessions?

Did the Egyptians give them anything?

How many men fled Egypt no including women and children?

How long had the Hebrews been in Egypt before they were finally freed?

Exodus 12:41-51

Could foreigners eat the Passover?

What had to be done before a servant could participate in the Passover?

Exodus 13:1-10

Who spoke to Moses once they departed?

Who was to be sanctified to the Lord?

Who were some of the inhabitants of the land where God was going to settle the Hebrews?

Exodus 13:11-22

Give a summary paragraph of verses 11-22.

Exodus 14:1-10

Where tell Moses to instruct the children to camp?

Did God know what Pharaoh would say?

Who hardened Pharaoh's heart?

What was God's objective in hardening Pharaoh's heart?

What happened that caused the Pharaoh to change his mind/heart?

How many chariots were commissioned to chase the children of Israel?

When the children of Israel saw the Egyptians what did they say to Moses?

Exodus 14:11-20

How did Moses respond to them?

While Moses was praying or crying-out to the Lord, what did God say to him?

What did God instruct Moses to do?

What was God's purpose to harden the pharaoh's heart?

What did the angel of the Lord do?

Exodus 14: 21-30

What happened, when Moses stretched out his hand over the sea?

What did the children of Israel do?

How did pharaoh's army respond?

What did God cause among the Egyptians?

What was the condition of the land, which was covered by water when the children of Israel walked upon it?

Where did the children of Israel see the Egyptians lying?

Exodus 15:1-10

After their victory, what did Moses and the sons of Israel do?

Provide some of the lyrics Moses and the Hebrews composed.

Exodus 15:11-20

What or where were the gods from whom the children of Israel compared to the almighty God?

What nations were intimidated by the Israelites liberation from Egypt?

According to the people, who would reign forever?

What did Miriam and the other women do?

Exodus 15:21-30

Where did the people go once they departed from the Red Sea?

Why couldn't the people drink the waters of Marah?

What did the people say?

How did Moses respond to their request?

What did God promise to do if the people followed His commandments?

Exodus 16:1-10

What did the Hebrews continue to do on the 15th day of the second month after their departure?

What did the Lord say to Moses concerning food?

Concerning their grumblings, Moses told the people that their grumblings were against who?

What happened when Aaron spoke to the whole congregation as they looked toward the wilderness?

Exodus 16:11-20

After hearing their grumbling what did God promise that He would provide for the Children of Israel?

When the Hebrews saw the fine frost or manna what question did they ask?

What did Moses say that it was?

How much did each person gather?

What did Moses tell the people not to do with the food?

How did the people respond to Moses' command?

Exodus 16:21-30

How much of the food did they gather on the sixth day?

Why did they gather more on the sixth day?

Did the excess food spoil as it did before?

Did anyone go out on the seventh day to find food?

Based on your opinion, describe the characteristics of these people toward God.

Exodus 16:31-36

What were the people to do with a portion of the manna for future generations?

How long did the Hebrews eat manna?

Exodus 17:1-10

Why did the people begin quarreling with Moses again?

Who did Moses turn to concerning their complaints?

Had this happened before?

What did God command Moses to do?

At any time during their travel to the promised land, did the Hebrews have to fight?

If so, who did they fight?

Is so, what does this tell us about God's promises to us?

Exodus 17:11-16

As they battled, what determine when the children of Israel were winning?

Who helped Moses?

How did they help him?

Did the children of Israel win?

What did Moses name the alter he built?

Exodus 18:1-10

Who was Jethro, and what did he hear about God?

What was Moses' wife's name?

Moses had two boys, Gershom and Eliezar, what does their names mean?

After Moses told his father-in law all that God had done, what was Jethro's response?

Exodus 18:21-27

What else was Moses to do organizationally to help himself?

Who actually was commanding Moses to use the approach recommended by Jethro?

What issues would the judges bring before Moses?

Exodus 19:1-10

How many months passed since the children of Israel left Egypt?

What object did God use to get Moses attention?

Did God make a promise to the children of Israel? If so, what did they have to do, AND what would God do in exchange?'

Exodus 19:21-25

What warning did Moses have for the people?

Who was to return with Moses?

Exodus 20:1-10

What was the first thing God reminded them?

What was God's position concerning any other god's?

What did God say about idols?

What will God do to fathers who hate Him?

What will God do for those who love Him and his commandments?

What will God do to persons who use His name in vain or without a sincere purpose?

How is the Sabbath day to be remembered?

Exodus 20:11-20

What did God do in the first six days according to Exo. 20:11?

What is promised when a believer honors his father and mother?

☐ True
☐ False

According to the commandments, is murder acceptable.

What is adultery, and is it prohibited.

What is bearing false witness.

What is the name of the preceding laws? *Hint: (The _____)*

What did the people do when they saw the thundering and lightning?

What did the people ask Moses to do for them?

What did Moses explain to the people?

Exodus 20: 21-26

What did God re-emphasize to the people through Moses?

Exodus 21:1-10

Were additional laws provided beyond the Ten Commandments?

How many years could a Hebrew remain enslaved by a fellow Hebrew?

If his master gives him a wife, who does the wife and children belong to after the slave is freed?

What happens if the Hebrew slave desires to remain with his master and family?

Were female slaves treated differently from male slaves?

How is the master to treat the female slave if the master gives her to his daughter?

If a master take another woman or wife, what three things must he continue to provide for his slave woman?

Exodus 21:11-20

If he does not provide for his enslaved woman, what is she free to do?

What happens to a person who strikes and kills another person?

What provision did God make for an accidental murder, or a murder that was not intended?

What was the penalty for a person who strikes his mother or father?

What was the penalty for kidnapping?

What was the penalty for cursing one's father or mother?

What happens if two men quarrel and one injures the other?

Exodus 21:31-40

If a master hit a servant and the servant did not die, what is the punishment?

If the servant lives a few days, then what was the punishment?

What's the penalty if men are fighting and they accidentally cause a woman to have a miscarriage?

What is the penalty if the baby is lost, and the woman is also injured?

If a master caused a servant to lose an eye or tooth, what would happen to the servant? What about the master?

If an ox gores a man or woman to death, is the owner held responsible?

If the ox had a history of goring, and gores someone to death what is the punishment?

What if a ransom is preferred by the family of the injured party instead of death. Is this lawful?

Exodus 21:31-36

Did it make any difference whether the victim was male or female?

How much was a servant worth who was killed by an ox?

According to laws concerning oxen, if one fell in a stranger's pit, what did the Law require?

Exodus 23:21-33

What did God promise if the Hebrews obeyed the angel of the Lord?

What were the Hebrews instructed to do to the inhabitants of the land?

If the Hebrews served the Lord, what did God promise them?

What was God going to send ahead of the Hebrews to drive out the Hivites, Canaanites, and Hittites?

[Biblical insight] Who is the most well known Hittite that you know?

What was the boundary of the promised land?

Once the Hebrews were successful, could they allow the defeated nations to live among them?

Exodus 24:1-10

When Moses told the people all of the ordinances, how did they respond?

After reading the book of the covenant, what did Moses use to certify the covenant?

Exodus 24:11-18

Who went up the mountain with Moses to receive the law and commandment?

Did the other elders go along with Moses and Joshua up the mountain?

What was the name of the mountain?

How long was Moses on the mountain?

Exodus 25:1-10

What were the sons of Israel to do for God?

What was used for anointing oil?

Name the two things they were to construct.

Exodus 25:11-20

What was used to overlay the ark?

How was the ark carried?

What was inside the ark?

What was placed on top of the ark?

What was constructed on the sides of the ark?

Are cherubim statues of animals?

Where the faces of the cherubim turned away from the mercy seat?
Exodus 25:21-30

What was God's position when he spoke?

How often would the Bread of Presence be presented to the Lord?

Exodus 25:31-40

What would provide light in the tabernacle?

☐ True
☐ False

God was not very detailed about what he wanted constructed.

Snuffers and trays were to be of pure gold.

Exodus 26:1-10

The tabernacle was comprised of ten curtains.

☐ True
☐ False

God was not particular about the skill level of the worker.

☐ True
☐ False

What were the builders to do with goat's hair.

Exodus 26:21-30

The west side of the tabernacle was constructed with six boards.

☐ True
☐ False

The boards were overlaid with gold.

☐ True
☐ False

The tabernacle was to be erected according to its plan.

☐ True
☐ False

Exodus 26:31-37

A veil was constructed of blue, purple, and scarlet material.

☐ True
☐ False

The veil was hung up and the ark was placed behind it.

☐ True
☐ False

The veil separated the holy place from the holy of holies.

    ☐ True
    ☐ False

The mercy seat on the ark was place outside of the holy of holies.

    ☐ True
    ☐ False

A screen was used for the doorway of the tent.

    ☐ True
    ☐ False

Five pillars of acacia were used for the screen.

    ☐ True
    ☐ False

Exodus 27:1-10

The altar was made of iron.

    ☐ True
    ☐ False

Horns were placed on the four corners of the alter.

    ☐ True
    ☐ False

The grating was made of wood.

    ☐ True
    ☐ False

Poles were constructed on two sides of the altar.

☐ True
☐ False

There was a court in the tabernacle.

☐ True
☐ False

Exodus 27:11-21

The width of the west and east side of the court was 50 cubits.

☐ True
☐ False

All the pillars around the court were furnished with sofas.

☐ True
☐ False

Clear oil from olives was used to fuel the lamp.

☐ True
☐ False

Aaron and his brothers were to keep things in order.

☐ True
☐ False

Exodus 28:1-10

Aaron's garments were made for glory and beauty.

☐ Truc
☐ False

Aaron was to minister as an evangelist?

☐ True
☐ False

Aaron's garments included a robe, crown, and haberdasher.

☐ True
☐ False

Two onyx stones were engraved with the names of the sons of Israel.

☐ True
☐ False

Exodus 28:11-20

Two stones were placed on the shoulder pieces of the ephod.

☐ True
☐ False

The breastpiece of judgment could be constructed by a novice.

☐ True
☐ False

Exodus 28:21-20

The breast pieces also had chains of twisted metal.

☐ True
☐ False

Aaron carried the names of the sons of Israel in the breastpiece of judgment over his heart.

☐ True
☐ False

Urim and Thummim were also in the breastpiece of judgment.

☐ True
☐ False

Aaron was to wear the breast piece continually

☐ True
☐ False

Exodus 28:31-43

The ephod was to be on Aaron when he ministered.

☐ True
☐ False

There was to be a gold plate with "Holy to the Lord" engraved on it.

☐ True
☐ False

The plate was to be attached to a turban and placed on Aaron's head.

☐ True
☐ False

Aaron's sons also had special wardrobes.

☐ True
☐ False

Exodus 29:1-10

What animals was Moses to use to consecrate Aaron and his sons?

Where was Moses to wash Aaron and his sons?

After Moses placed the turban and crown on Aaron's head, what followed?

After ordaining Aaron and his sons, what did Aaron and his sons touch with their hands?

Exodus 29:11-20

The bull was to be slaughtered.

☐ True
☐ False

The fat was offered up in smoke.

☐ True
☐ False

The bulls hide and refuse was burned later in the camp.

☐ True
☐ False

Two rams were also offered.

☐ True
☐ False

One ram was used as a burnt offering.

☐ True
☐ False

The other ram was used as a blood offering.

    ☐ True
    ☐ False

The blood from the ram was only sprinkled around the altar.

    ☐ True
    ☐ False

Exodus 29:21-30

Both blood and the anointing oil were sprinkled on Aaron's garments.

    ☐ True
    ☐ False

The fat of the ram, one cake of bread, one cake of bread mixes, and other wafers were used as a wave offering.

    ☐ True
    ☐ False

The breast of Aaron's ram was used as a wave offering.

    ☐ True
    ☐ False

The holy garments of Aaron shall be for his sons after him, that in them they may be anointed and ordained.

    ☐ True
    ☐ False

Exodus 29:31-40

The ram of ordination was buried.

    ☐ True
    ☐ False

Aaron and his sons were to eat the meat of the ram.

☐ True
☐ False

Laypersons could not eat the things used to consecrate the ministers.

☐ True
☐ False

Atonement for sin was made daily.

☐ True
☐ False

Exodus 30:1-10

Where was the alter to be located?

What was Aaron to burn on the altar?

What was the duration of the incense before the Lord?

How often was Aaron commanded to make atonement?

Exodus 30:11-20

When Moses took a census, what was each son of Israel to give?

Regardless of wealth, how much was each person to pay?

How was the atonement money used?

What were Aaron and his sons to do upon entering the tent meeting?

Exodus 30:31-37

Could this anointing oil be poured on anyone's body?

What ingredients were used for the incense?

Could the incense be made in the same proportions for the priests?

Exodus 31:1-10

What did the Lord call Bezaleel to do?

Who else did the Lord call to prepare the articles and wardrobes of the tabernacle?

Exodus 31:11-18

How was the anointing oil and incense to be made?

What day was important to observe?

What would happen to the person who worked on the Sabbath?

What reason did God give for observing the Sabbath?

[Spiritual insight] Now, as a Christian, what does the Bible say about the Sabbath day (see Colossians 2:16-17; 20-22)

Exodus 32:1-10

When Moses delayed coming down the mountain, what did the people request?

What did Aaron instruct them to do?

What was Aaron's part in creating the idol?

What did God tell Moses to do?

When Moses spoke to Pharaoh, God told Moses to tell Pharaoh to let "My people" go. When the people were disobedient, whose people were they (see vs. 7)?

What did God say about the people?

And what was God going to do?

Exodus 32:11-20

Who interceded on behalf of the people?

What did Moses have with him as he descended the mountain?

When Joshua heard all of the noise, what did he think?

When Moses arrived near the camp what did he do?

Exodus 32:21:30

Who did Moses speak with first?

Did Aaron tell the truth about how the calf appeared?

Who allowed the people to get out of control?

When Moses requested volunteers who came to his side?

What did Moses instruct them to do?

What did Moses tell the people the next day?

Exodus 32:31-35

What did Moses admit to God?

What did Moses ask God to do?

What existed that apparently had names?

Would God allow Moses to substitute for the punishment of the people?

Exodus 33:1-10

After the golden calf incident, did God forgive the people?

What did God instruct Moses to do afterwards?

Who was going to drive out the inhabitants of the land promised to the Hebrews?

What was some of the resources in this land?

Exodus 33:11-23

Characterize how God spoke to Moses.

Who stayed at the tent when Moses returned to the camp?

What did Moses desire to know about God?

What was Moses' request if God was not going to be present with him?

How does God choose who will be the recipient of His graciousness?

The scripture (vs. 11) said Moses spoke with God face to face, but (vs. 20) says no man can see God's face and live. So what do you think all of this means?

What did the Lord do with Moses while His glory passed by?

What part of God was Moses allowed to see?

Exodus 34:1-10

What did God instruct Moses to do for a second time?

Was anyone to ascend the mountain with Moses?

What happened while Moses was calling on the name of the Lord?

What did the Lord say about Himself?

What did Moses do quickly?

What did Moses request?

What did God promise that he would do?

Exodus 34:11-20

Again, what did God promise that He would do to the inhabitants in the Promised Land?

What did God forbid His people to do with the inhabitants of the land?

[Spiritual Insight] Why did God want the Hebrews to destroy everything belonging to the inhabitants of the land?

What were the Hebrews to be sure to give to the Lord?

Exodus 34:21-30

Again, what were the Hebrews to do concerning work and rest?

What was the Feast of Weeks?

How often were males to appear before the Lord?

What was God going to do with their borders?

What was not to be offered at the same time?

What did the Lord instruct Moses to do concerning His words?

How long was Moses there, and what did he abstain from during this period?

When Moses came down the mountain, what would he find the people doing?

When the people saw Moses, how did they respond?

Exodus 34:31-35

What would Moses do when he finished speaking with the congregation?

What would he do whenever he went before the Lord?

Why would Moses use the veil?

Exodus 35:1-10

Concerning the Sabbath, what was the congregation to do?

Concerning contributions, how was a contributor to bring an offering to the Lord?

What quality did Moses require for the person who would help to construct and sew materials?

Exodus 35:11-20

What was to be constructed to complete the tabernacle?

What was to be constructed to complete the ark?

What was to be constructed to complete the lamp stand?

Describe some other things requiring completion.

Exodus 35:31-35

Who did God fill with His Spirit?

What did God empower them to do?

What else did he put into their hearts?

Exodus 36:1-10

Whose instructions did these skillful craftsmen have to follow?

What "good" problem did the craftsmen discover?

As a result, what did Moses do?

Exodus 36:11-20

What was the material, which made up the tent over the tabernacle?

What materials were used to cover the boards of the tabernacle?

Exodus 36: 21-30

What was the length of each board?

How many boards were on the south side?

How many boards were there for the north side?

Exodus 36:31-38

What material was used to overlay the boards?

What was the color of the veil?

Exodus 37:1-10

What material was used to overlay the poles?

What were the poles used to do?

What was on both ends of the mercy seat?

Exodus 37: 11-20

What was under the first pair of branches?

What material was used to make the lamps and stuffers?

What material was used to overlay the poles?

What was the compound of the anointing oil?

Exodus 38:1-10

What was the material of the altar for the burnt offering?

What material was used for each horn on the altar?

What material was used for the south side?

Exodus 38:11-20

Give a brief description of the pillars.

Give a brief description of the hangings.

Exodus 38:21-31

What was the complete name of the tabernacle?

Did the artisans finish the task?

What did the bekah head represent?

Exodus 39:1-10

What else was made from the blue, purple, and scarlet material?

Who would wear these garments?

Exodus 39:11-20

Who did the stones represent?

Exodus 39:21-30

What connected the breastplate and ephod?

What color was the priest's robe?

What color were the ornaments around the garment?

What was located on the hem of the garment?

What did they prepare for their heads?

Exodus 39:31-40

Who commanded all of the detail instructions for the priest's clothing?

Did the sons of Israel do all they were commanded to do concerning the tabernacle, clothing, and ornaments?

What color was the rams' skin dyed?

After Moses examined all the work, what did he do?

Exodus 40: 1-10

What was Moses to do on the first day of the first month?

What was used as a screen for the ark?

What was Moses to do with the anointing oil?

Exodus 40:11-20

Who was Moses to wash?

Who along with Aaron was Moses to anoint?

What was the duration of their priesthood?

What was used to erect the tabernacle?

What did Moses place inside the ark?

What was on top of the ark?

Exodus 40:21-30

What did Moses place within the tabernacle first?

What did Moses set in order on the table?

After lighting the lamps, what did Moses do next?

Exodus 40:31-40

What parts of their anatomy did Moses and his relatives wash?

As they approached the alter, what did they do?

What did the cloud do once Moses was finished with the tabernacle?

Why couldn't Moses enter the tent of meeting?

What would the people do whenever the cloud left the tabernacle?

What was leading the people throughout their journeys?

Printed in the United States
130115LV00003B/93/A

9 781932 672299